A fun, flavorful cookbook with more than 95 recipes and Power-Ups featuring chef Mason Hereford's irreverent take on Southern food, from his awarding-winning New Orleans restaurant Turkey and the Wolf.

Mason Hereford grew up in rural Virginia, where his formative meals came at modest country stores and his family's holiday table. After moving to New Orleans and working in fine dining he opened Turkey and the Wolf, which featured his larger-than-life interpretations of down-home dishes and created a nationwide sensation.

In *Turkey and the Wolf*, Hereford shares lively twists on beloved Southern dishes, like potato chip–loaded fried bologna sandwiches, deviled-egg tostadas with salsa macha, and his mom's burnt tomato casserole. This cookbook is packed with nostalgic and indulgent recipes, original illustrations, and bad-ass photographs.

Filled with recipes designed to get big flavor out of laidback cooking, *Turkey and the Wolf* is a wild ride through the South, with food so good you're gonna need some brand-new jeans.

Turkey AND THE WOLF

MASON HEREFORD
WITH JJ GOODE

Photographs by William Hereford
Illustrations by Leo Gonzales
Lettering by Ashlee Arceneaux Jones

Turkey AND THE WOLF

FLAVOR TRIPPIN' IN NEW ORLEANS

TEN SPEED PRESS
California | New York

To the late Robert Hereford,
my old man and my best friend

CONTENTS

1 Introduction

1 | A MONTH OF SUNDAYS
BREAKFAST

14 **Deviled-Egg Tostadas**

17 **Colleen's Bagel Bites**

18 **Collards and Grits with Salsa Macha**

21 **Don't Sleep on the Carrot Yogurt**

25 **Molly's Biscuits**

30 **Grand Slam McMuffin**

32 **Meatloaf: The Bagel, Not the Musician**

2 | THE SALAD RANCH
SALAD

39 **Buffalo Waldorf Salad**

42 **The Cabbage Patch**

47 **Leftover Fried Chicken Salad**

50 **Sunday Morning Coming-Down Potato Salad**

53 **The Wedge**

57 **Lamb, Peas, Mint, and Cereal Salad**

3 | BIG HAT, NO CATTLE
VEGETABLES

61 **Sweet Potato Burrito**

62 **Roasted Sunchoke and White Truffle Dunkaroos**

65 **White Bean Hummus with Chile-Crunch Peas**

67 **Gas-Station Tostadas**

71 **Visualize Whirled Peas on Toast**

75 **Okranomiyaki**

4 | DELTA FOLLY
SOME SEAFOOD

79 Catfish Blues

82 Crab Cake Muffs

85 Roe a la Jiffy

86 Lobster Tostadas

91 Hot Tuna

94 McCaviar

97 Shrimp with Grapes and Nuts

5 | ENJOY EVERY SANDWICH
SANDWICHES

104 The Bellair (The Reason We Make Sandwiches)

106 The Collard Melt

109 The 86'd Chicken-Fried Steak

116 The Tomato

119 The Italian-American

123 The Softshell Crab

126 The Bologna

129 Meatloaf: The Sandwich, Not the Musician

6 | SHAKE HANDS WITH BEEF
DISHES FOR MEAT LOVERS

133 Chicken Potpies That Fit in Your Pocket

137 Corner-Store Pork Rind Tacos

139 Fried Chicken Skins and Deviled Eggs

143 Spicy Fried Chicken Salad on Roti Paratha

145 Slow-Cooked Lamb Necks with Fixings on Roti Paratha

147 Hog's Head Cheese

153 Hog's Head Cheese Rice

154 Hog's Head Cheese Tacos

157 Hog's Head Cheese Collards

161 Grocery-Store Tonnato Sauce

7 | SIDE HUSTLE
FIXINGS

165   **Mom's Famous Burnt Tomatoes**

167   **Buttermilk Mashed Potatoes**

171   **My Best Attempt at Anne Hereford's Apple Fritters**

172   **Mason's Danksgiving Day Puree**

176   **Used to Call It Stuffing, Now I Call It Dressing**

178   **Scotty's Good-with-Everything Collard Greens**

181   **There Should Probably Be a Salad (Caesar)**

8 | MAMA TRIED
BURGER-JOINT FARE

184   **The Mama Tried Burger**

186   **Dan Stein as a Hot Dog**

191   **Via's Corn Dogs with Her Mom's Mustard**

192   **Not Yo Mama's Peanut Butter–Bacon Burger**

194   **Spicy Chicken Thigh Roaster Sandwich**

9 | JUST LIQUOR & DESSERT FROM HERE ON OUT
DESSERTS

202   **No-Churn Ice Cream Sundae**

205   **Beet Butter and Tahini on Ice Cream**

206   **Magic Shell and Potato Stix on Ice Cream**

209   **Crunk Chunks on Ice Cream**

210   **Candied Peanuts, Nutter Butters, and Toasted Coconut on Ice Cream**

213   **Cheez-Its and Peanuts on Ice Cream**

10 | WHEN I DIP, YOU DIP, WE DIP
DIPS, SPREADS & OTHER STUFF

216 **Verdant Blender Sauce**

217 **Tay's Mustard**

218 **Bellair-Style Herb Mayo**

219 **Peanut Butter
Salsa Macha**

222 **Halfway-Homemade
Hot Sauce**

223 **Pizza Cream Cheese**

224 **Anchovy Crème Fraîche**

225 **Spicy Russian Dressing**

226 **Big Zesty Buttermilk
Dressing**

227 **Gas-Station Bean Dip**

228 **My Best Try at Colleen's
Onion Dip**

229 **Shrettuce**

230 **Nate's Spicy Chicken
Spices**

231 **Chicken Salt**

233 Acknowledgments

238 About the Authors

239 Index

INTRODUCTION

The story begins with a bad sandwich. I grew up in rural Virginia, in the tiny town of Free Union. My formative food experiences were at shabby, family-run country stores—part gas station, part convenience mart, and part takeout counter. They sold beer and gas, lures and ammo, chili-cheese dogs and biscuits with white gravy. Some sold the delicacy that my mom calls "rat cheese," a wheel of fake cheddar that sweats all day on the counter, typically unwrapped and unrefrigerated, to be purchased by the hunk and eaten with some saltines. It's the dairy equivalent of a loosie cigarette.

Sometimes when we were hard up for lunch, we'd stop at one of these stores and my mom would grab us some bologna sandwiches. I hated those bologna sandwiches. I hated the texture of flabby off-brand cased meat. I hated the yellow mustard (which I couldn't stomach unless, for some reason, it was on a McDonald's burger). The only way I knew how to turn that sandwich into something worth eating was to load it with salt-and-vinegar potato chips. Never would've guessed that some twenty years later, my version of that bologna sandwich would be featured in magazines, on food TV shows, and, most important, in a mayonnaise commercial.

Mostly, though, I loved the food in those stores. There's Wyant's, in White Hall, Virginia, which has been run by the Wyant family since 1888 and where the sausage biscuit never fails to hit the spot. There's Brownsville Market, in Crozet, which has a hot case stocked with broccoli-cheese casserole and fried chicken. And there's Bellair Market, in Charlottesville, where every week for a decade, I ordered a sandwich called The Jefferson: turkey, cheddar, and cranberry relish on a French roll, slathered with an herb mayo that shows up in my dreams (and on page 104).

The store that had the biggest influence on the way I cook today didn't make food at all. Maupin Brothers Store was a few minutes by foot from our shabby A-frame in Free Union. We went every day, often several times a day. We were there so much that it became like an extension of our home. Della Maupin (we all called her "Miss Maupin"); her husband, Kemper; and their son Mike ran the

1

store. They let my mom run a big tab. They ratted out my brother when he pulled my mom's rusty GMC Suburban into their parking lot before he had his license. They were family.

The most memorable times were in the mornings. Mom had to get four kids ready for school, and when we missed the bus, which happened hilariously often, she would cram us in the GMC, spill coffee on herself, then make a beeline to Maupin's. She'd let the truck idle in the lot and set us loose in the aisles. Some days, I'd grab a Jimmy Dean sausage biscuit or bean burrito plucked from the freezer case and thaw it to perfection in the microwave. Other days, I'd pop open a can of jalapeño-flavored Vienna sausage, because even as a young kid I had a very refined palate. Often, I opted for an ensemble breakfast: a bag of Doritos, a Snickers bar, and a can of Mr. Pibb. I always tried to make the food last the entire drive, and the ultimate was pulling up to school as I took my last bites—two Doritos at once followed by the center cut from the Snickers chased by the final sip of Pibb.

Junk food wasn't my only muse. My fancy grandma, who asked us to call her Ann, was a badass cook: I'm talking game birds, duck fricassee, and snapper with herbed lemon butter. My mom still has Ann's dictionary-thick recipe book, a hodgepodge of newspaper clippings and handwritten instructions. My mom also has her own mother's recipe book. Her mom's name is Anne, too, but she always went by Grandmommy. Grandmommy is as country as Ann was high-falutin. Her book is full of recipes, like cornpone, kraut dumplings, and hickory-nut loaf cake, written in her looped scrawl on paper that's now yellowed and cracked. While Ann was making sure her table was set with the proper flatware, Grandmommy was rolling by the fridge to snack on raw hamburger meat sprinkled with salt and pepper.

My mom cooked food that was somewhere in between. It wasn't fancy, and it reflected the same sort of practical considerations that brought me to Maupin's for breakfast. She made an amazing dish of chicken with evaporated milk and apple juice concentrate. She melted American cheese on broccoli to serve with frozen fish sticks, and used Rice Krispies as a crust for baked chicken thighs. She made a special-occasion chicken curry with peas that would rock me every time. Then there were burnt tomatoes: a kind of magical casserole made from sliced, flour-dredged, pan-fried tomatoes that are sprinkled with sugar and baked to hell. She still makes them for

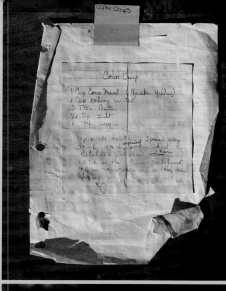

Thanksgiving every year, and even though her son, the chef, cooks the rest of the meal, her burnt tomatoes are always the best thing on the table.

Still, I definitely didn't have designs on being a chef. Right after college, I moved down to New Orleans, which I knew practically on arrival would be my forever home, and realized pretty quickly that I wasn't going to be using my art history degree. My first job was as a door guy (think Swayze in *Road House*) at Fat Harry's, a bar in Uptown. A few months later I became a cook there, and eventually a really crappy bartender—top of the totem pole, as far as the money was concerned.

That's where I learned to cook—making burgers for the oddball regulars and cheese fries for the budding alcoholics at Tulane and Loyola. It was there, among the deep fryers and endless shots of Grand Marnier, where I became entranced by the alchemy of cooking, by how a little mustard wash, flour, and bird meat could enter a vat of bubbling oil and emerge as chicken fingers. When it was slow, the manager, Joey, would teach me all sorts of cool stuff that was definitely not on the menu, like how to fry soft-shell crabs and make barbecue-shrimp pistolettes. At some point I realized, cash tips be damned, I wanted to cook.

After a year at Fat Harry's, I scored a job as a line cook at Coquette, a cool bistro in the Garden District that crushed at turning local meat and produce into inventive Southern food. I stuck around for six years. By the time I became Coquette's chef de cuisine, I had learned to do some pretty neat chef shit, like taking modest stuff, like fried chicken or catfish, and dressing it up, and taking fancy-sounding stuff, like veal sweetbreads or beef tartare, and dressing it down.

Creative freedom and youthful enthusiasm kept me going despite years of eighty-hour work weeks peppered with hangovers, eating over trash cans, and broken cigarettes. Yet what actually got me through it was the people, the post-work revelry, the realization that we had all somehow found jobs that let us pay our rent without really growing up. I don't remember, for instance, the choreography that allowed five grown adults in a tiny kitchen to put out hundreds of meticulous plates on busy nights. But I will never forget the fun: the time my fellow cook and close pal Richard Horner woke up after his first Mardi Gras with a mysterious pain in his shoulder, which turned out to be a tattoo that read "Kara Anderson is Hot

Sauce"—even though he can't remember ever meeting Kara. Still, she did friend him on Facebook months later. Needless to say, he was late to work that day. Or the time some silly goose sucked down a whippit from the iSi gun that we employed to make foamed horseradish cream, right before the Friday dinner rush, and brought the kitchen to its knees for a spell. (Again, I'm sorry to everyone who worked or waited too long for their food that night.) Or how every Sunday night, we'd meet at the bar down the street and stay for hours and hours after they locked the doors for last call, talking loud, ripping cigs, and dancing to Sugar Hill Gang, as if we hadn't just put in fifteen hours on our feet. These were the same friends who joined me when I set out to open my own place, which we decided would be as much about serving good food as it was about bringing the party to work and figuring out how never to do another fifteen-hour day ever again.

Back in August 2016, I opened a restaurant called Turkey and the Wolf, a few blocks from that bar, in the Irish Channel. "Turkey" was what my old man called us kids when we were being little fuckers. "Wolf" came from the howls that went up from the kitchen at Coquette after we sent out the night's final dish. I partnered up

with Lauren Holton, my girlfriend at the time, whose name I have tattooed on my ass. We broke up, but don't worry, my wife's name is also Lauren and now my ass says "New Lauren."

Turkey and the Wolf is an enthusiastically casual spot. The food comes on vintage Disney, Power Rangers, and Ronald McDonald plates we found on eBay. People sit on chairs and at tables that my mom found at yard sales. We have only ten or so items on the menu at any given time. Most of them are sandwiches, and there is no governing principle other than we serve what we think tastes good: hog's head cheese tacos with shredded iceberg and American cheese, a collard green sandwich that tastes like a Reuben, a bagel-inspired wedge salad, and an adorable fried chicken potpie that would fit in your pocket.

In our merry misfit kitchen crew was Colleen—master of dips, hater of olives, culinary school crusher with an awesome bandana collection destined for greatness. There was Nate—talks slow, thinks fast, and a while back moved from frying catfish to wood-firing prime meats for the wealthy and it almost killed him, though not for lack of talent. He recently started wearing a gold chain (it's a good look). There was Scotty—prep wiz, former competitive bike messenger, infamous multitasker, and master of collard green cookery. There was Swade—a great dancer who started his culinary journey around the corner cooking shrimp po'boys at Parasol's, barfed when I took him to Houston, and let the kitchen crew name his son. There was Migdalia—faster than the rest and a selfless goddess who might also threaten to break your twig legs if you get in her way, whose family owns pigs and who often reminds Nate he looks a bit like them. And there was Kate, who was briefly a boutique dog-clothing salesperson before managing restaurants and joined our team to do anything but manage and then became our general manager. We were all there from the start and we're still together today.

Nowadays, we take a more direct route to deliciousness than we used to at our fine-dining jobs. Instead of toiling to make some braised short rib appetizer taste like someone turned a Slim Jim into a pig in a blanket, we'd probably just serve a fuckin' Slim Jim pig in a blanket. The energy spared goes right into making that straightforward food even more fun. We still apply all the tools we once used to build and combine flavors but to create food that wouldn't feel entirely out of place in one of those country stores I went to all the time as a kid.

Our hope when we opened was that some people would come by and try our food. Then they did and things got a bit out of hand. Before we hit the year mark, we were on a bunch of "Best of" lists and got so busy we were burning through the next day's prep so fast we'd have to shut down early to avoid prepping late into the night. We had a good run as the world's most overrated sandwich shop, before the mob turned back into a more manageable party. We still had a blast pretty much the entire time.

Now, I've got two restaurants, Turkey and the Wolf and a breakfast spot called Molly's Rise and Shine, named after my sister. I love cooking for people and I love the friends I get to cook with. We all finish work by 4 or 5 p.m. but typically don't stop hanging and occasionally causing mischief till 6 or 7. And we've been cranking out high times and fun food long enough that the big shots in New York gave us the green light for a cookbook. I'm excited that my mom can put this on her coffee table, where it'll look real nice, since my brother took the photos. I'm happy I got to write this book with my pal JJ, who once ate so much at Turkey and the Wolf that he clogged our toilet and is only telling me this just now, three years after the

plunging. And I'm grateful that when the opportunity came, the talented friends I met during a dozen years of working in kitchens together showed up to help me make the thing special.

I hope you like what we made, too. This book contains recipes for food I love that you can reasonably make at home or, in the case of one recipe that requires a pig's head and a good sixteen hours of your time, that you should strongly consider making at home even if it almost takes you down. You'll find a bunch of favorites from Turkey and the Wolf and Molly's, and you'll also find some of the best dishes we've ever made at the restaurant but never made it on the menu because they didn't work logistically or didn't fit even within the capacious contours of our operations. You'll also find the kind of desserts I make at home, which require minimal baking because I don't know shit about baking.

What they all have in common is that they max out flavor and fun and ditch unnecessary work. They show that you can cut corners and still be proud of what you created. At the restaurant, for example, we make our own ham by brining pork legs for eight days and smoking them for ten hours, and we buy that pork from farmer friends, and the pigs have names and hobbies and lead happy lives, at least until the day they start down the road to ham. One reason we make our own is because we like to, but it's also cheaper than buying nice ham someone else made, and I'm trying to run a dang business. But you know who else has really good ham? The grocery store. You know what's better than your homemade mayonnaise? Duke's mayo. And anyway, the key to our kind of cooking isn't the ham or the mayo, but the way we combine it with other tasty stuff to make something we like to eat.

So as much as this book is about good food, it's about giving you permission to relax a little. You're allowed to make your own hot sauce by mixing together other hot sauces. You're allowed to doctor leftover Popeyes, hit the drive-thru for hash browns and then put stuff on them, or combine canned and jarred stuff to re-create the pleasures of the pop-top bean dip you used to get at the gas station. You shouldn't make an ingredient from scratch if a great version already exists unless making it sounds fun. Fun is the most important thing.

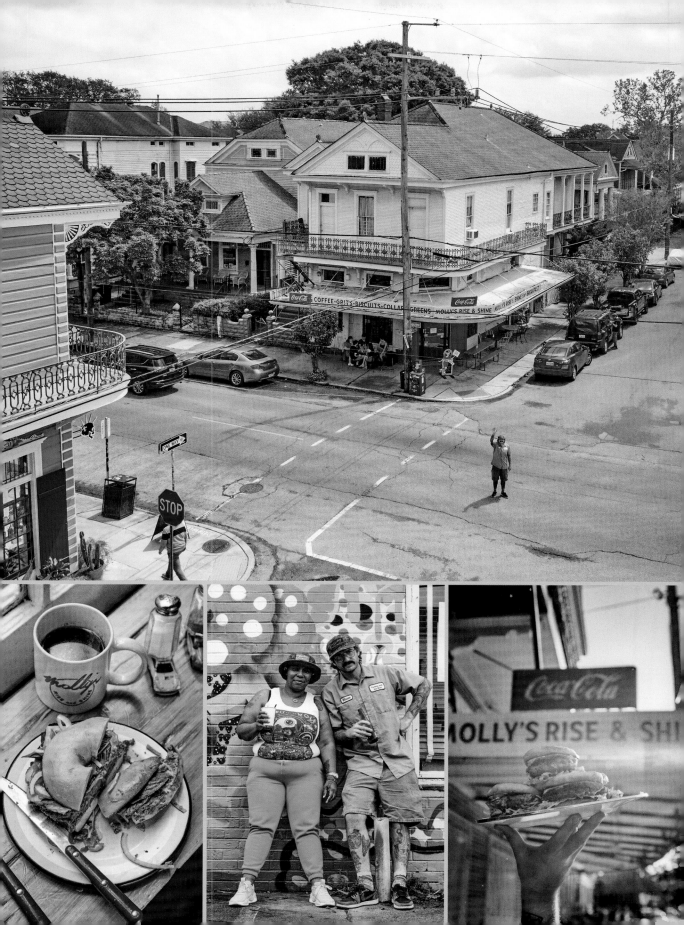

MAC FOLGER

COLLEEN QUARLS

BOB O'DONNELL

CHARLES ROACH

VIA FORTIER

NINI NGUYEN

RICHARD HORNER

CHRIS LORIO

MIGDALIA PABON

SCOTTY YELITY

WILL MONDROS

QUOC TRIEU

KATE MIRANTE

MICHAEL "SWADE" SWADENER

PHIL CENAC

NATHAN BARFIELD

MIRO HOFFMAN

SHAVON BANISTER

1
AMON
SUN
BREAKFAST

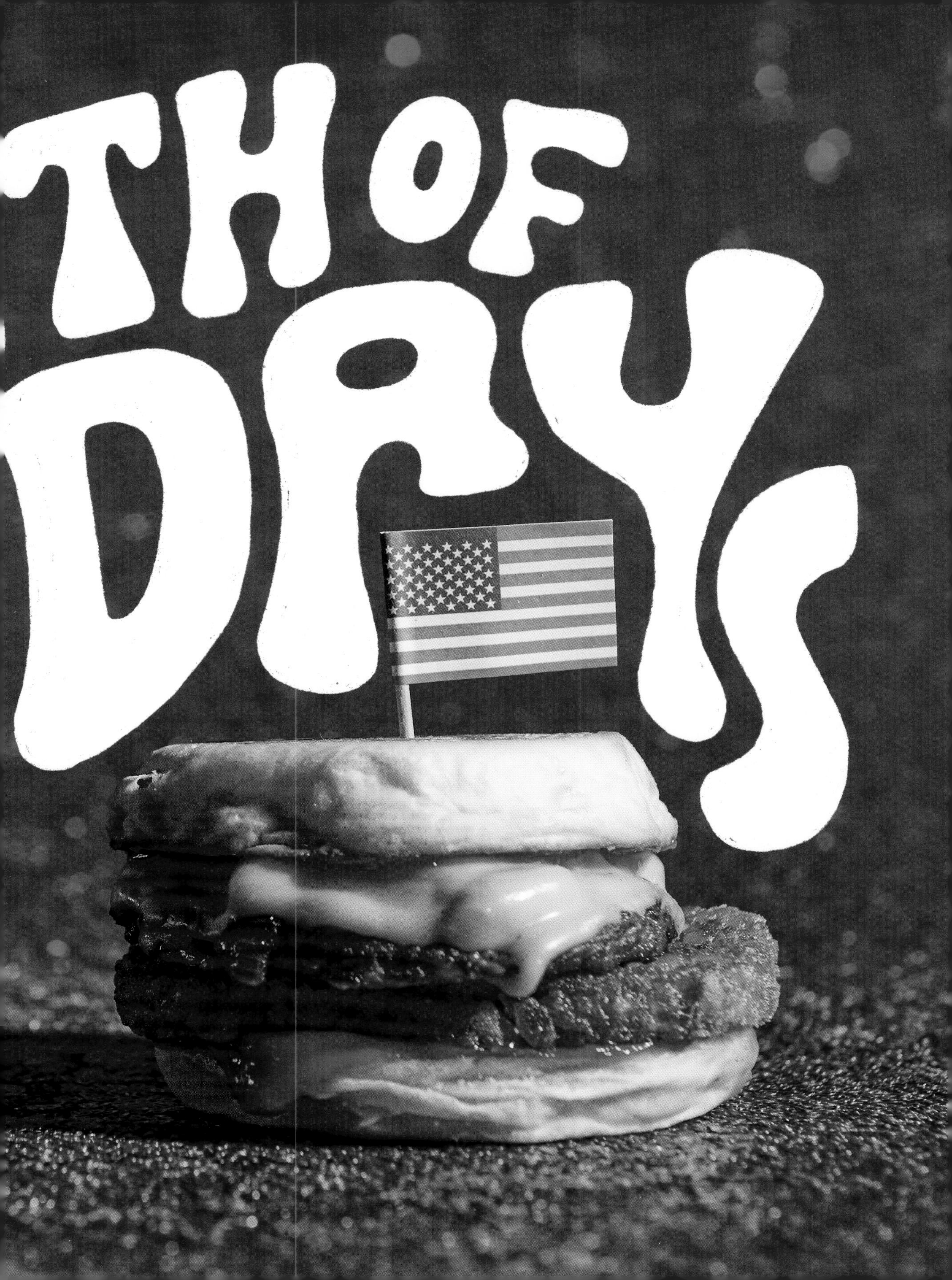
TH OF
DAYS

DEVILED-EGG TOSTADAS

When I was messing with the opening menu for Molly's Rise and Shine, I had fun thinking about what dishes qualify as breakfast. We hit the classics: biscuits, grits, breakfast sandwiches. We combined early-morning flavors from different places: labneh sprinkled with za'atar *and* everything-bagel spice. And we hallucinated: bagel chips with green cream cheese and canned sardines. And then there's, well, this. It's a dish that takes a time-tested Mexican formula (tostada, beans, tasty stuff, salsa) and applies the flavors of Southern picnics and roadside stores.

Assemble each one yourself, if you're feeling fancy, or set out the components and have everyone get involved.

To make the deviled yolks: In a food processor, process the yolks, sour cream, cheese, buttermilk, juice from half the lime, and salt to a smooth puree, about 30 seconds. Season with more lime juice and salt until you're happy, and gradually blend in a little more buttermilk if the mixture seems too thick to spread onto the tostadas.

To make the tostadas: Remove the bean dip from the fridge 10 to 15 minutes before you want to eat, so it softens up a bit for spreading. Evenly spread the deviled yolks across the tostadas (about 2 tablespoons each). Add some little dollops of the bean dip, about a tablespoon's worth per tostada.

Sprinkle on the banana peppers, onion, and then the cilantro. Use a Microplane to zest the limes over the tostadas, as evenly as you can. Halve a lime or two and squeeze them on. Spoon on that spicy-ass salsa macha, until you're happy. Eat.

MAKES 12

Deviled Yolks

Yolks from 12 hard-boiled eggs (feed the whites to your dog)

¼ cup plus 2 tablespoons sour cream

¼ cup plus 2 tablespoons finely crumbled cotija cheese

¼ cup plus 2 tablespoons well-shaken buttermilk, plus more if you need it

1 juicy lime, halved

½ teaspoon kosher salt (Diamond Crystal or about half as much Morton), or more if you like

Tostadas

¾ cup Gas-Station Bean Dip (page 227)

12 store-bought tostadas

¾ cup drained pickled banana pepper rings, roughly chopped

Some finely chopped red onion

1½ cups lightly packed roughly chopped cilantro

3 juicy limes, for zesting and juicing

Peanut Butter Salsa Macha (page 219) for serving

COLLEEN'S BAGEL BITES

In its short albeit storied history, Turkey and the Wolf went through a school-snacks phase, where we re-created heady, just barely more sophisticated versions of our nostalgic favorites. There were steak-and-cheese Hot Pockets, blood-sausage Lunchables (with an Andes Mint on the side), and Colleen's ode to Cheese & Pepperoni Bagel Bites. This one stuck around, though, because it's better than good. It's all about her thoughtfully rendered tomato cream cheese—at room temp, to make it and your joy more spreadable—paired with supermarket-quality pepperoni and a wild amount of toasted fennel seeds. Scale it up for a bigger party.

MAKES 12

3 tablespoons fennel seeds

6 tablespoons unsalted butter, room-temp so it's mayo-soft

6 plain bagels, halved

Heaping 1½ cups Pizza Cream Cheese (page 223), room-temp so it's nice and soft

1 tablespoon red chile flakes

4 ounces thinly sliced pepperoni (about 60 slices)

Big ol' handful of Italian basil leaves

Put the fennel seeds in a small skillet, set it over medium heat, and toast, shaking the pan frequently, until they're fragrant and a shade darker, about 3 minutes. Set them aside.

Get your oven to 400°F with a baking sheet in there.

Butter each bagel and, when the oven is ready, put them cut-side down on the hot baking sheet. Bake until the cut sides are golden brown, 5 to 7 minutes. Remove from the oven.

When the bagel halves are cool enough to handle, liberally smear the cream cheese on them. Sprinkle with the toasted fennel seeds and chile flakes, then top with the pepperoni and basil. Or put everything out and let people choose their own adventure.

COLLARDS AND GRITS WITH SALSA MACHA

The first time I tried salsa macha with collard greens, I knew we had a fun dish in the making. Turns out smoky, spicy, and nutty goes real well with rich, sweet, and vinegary. The marriage bed for this freaky couple is stone-ground grits made with butter and cream cheese. Go huge on the peanuts; they really tie the room together. Slip on some fried or poached eggs, if you want.

To make the grits: Combine the milk, salt, and 1½ cups water in a medium pot and bring to a boil over medium-high heat. Whisk the mixture with one hand and pour in the grits with the other; whisk constantly until it returns to a simmer, about 2 minutes. Turn down the heat to low so the grits simmer gently and cook, stirring occasionally, until they're tender, about 45 minutes. Don't worry if they look a little dry and sad. They won't in a minute.

Add the cream cheese, sour cream, butter, Tabasco, and pepper and whisk well to melt the butter and totally mix in the cream cheese. Add more salt and Tabasco until you're happy. Turn off the heat and cover to keep them warm, if necessary.

To assemble the dish: Spoon the grits into four bowls, then top with the collard greens (plus a little pot likker, if there is any hanging around). Spoon on some salsa macha, spreading it around to distribute the spiciness, then pile on the peanuts and sprinkle on the cilantro. Serve with the lime wedges.

SERVES 4

Grits

1½ cups whole milk

1½ teaspoons kosher salt (Diamond Crystal or about half as much Morton), or more if you like

¾ cup good stone-ground grits

Heaping ⅓ cup Philadelphia cream cheese, room-temp so it's nice and soft

¼ cup sour cream

3 tablespoons unsalted butter

2 teaspoons Tabasco jalapeño sauce, plus more for the freaks

¾ teaspoon freshly ground black pepper

For the Dish

3 cups Scotty's Good-with-Everything Collard Greens (page 178), hot

Peanut Butter Salsa Macha (page 219) for serving

¾ cup salted roasted peanuts, roughly chopped

¾ cup packed roughly chopped cilantro

4 lime wedges

DON'T SLEEP ON THE CARROT YOGURT

New customers at Molly's usually go for the fried chicken biscuit or Grand Slam McMuffin—after all, we opened the place hot off all the love for Turkey and the Wolf's meatwiches. But regulars know the deal. Our carrot yogurt is the sleeper hit on the menu. That's because it's got a sneaky carrot puree swirled in, Liz's carrot marmalade spooned on, and my buddy Nini Nguyen's granola on top, which I'm pretty sure she stole from a famous restaurant.

SERVES 4

Carrot Puree

2 cups sliced (about ½ inch) carrots

2 tablespoons maple syrup

1 teaspoon kosher salt (Diamond Crystal or about half as much Morton)

For the Dish

4 cups whole-milk Greek yogurt (or whatever you fuck with)

2 to 4 cups Nini's Granola (page 22) or your favorite one

1 cup or so blueberries (or whatever berries are ripe)

2 tangerines, clementines, or satsumas, peeled and separated into segments

Handful of mint leaves, torn

1 lemon, for zesting

Heaping 4 tablespoons Liz's Carrot Marmalade (page 23) or honey

To make the carrot puree: Put the carrots in a medium pot, cover with an inch of water, and get it boiling over high heat. Lower the heat and cook at a rolling simmer until the carrots are poke-a-finger-through-them tender, about 1 hour. (Sorry you burned your finger.) Use a slotted spoon to move the carrots to your blender, but don't ditch the water yet.

Add the maple syrup, salt, and just enough of the cooking water to get the blender moving (say, 3 tablespoons). Blend on high speed until totally smooth, about 1 minute. Let it cool and chill it in the fridge, where it'll keep in an airtight container for up to a week.

To assemble the dish: Plop the yogurt in bowls, add some or all of the carrot puree, and use a spoon to swirl it all around so it looks cool. Top each with ½ to 1 cup of the granola, some berries, citrus segments, and mint leaves. Zest the lemon over all the stuff and spoon the carrot marmalade over each bowl. It's ready to go.

NINI'S GRANOLA

Nini Nguyen taught us how to make this awesome granola before she became a food celebrity. If by some strange turn she isn't a celebrity by the time this is published, then just give it another few weeks. Makes about 7 cups

⅔ cup unsweetened shredded coconut

3 cups rolled oats

One 10½-ounce can (2 cups) salted roasted mixed nuts, roughly chopped

½ cup grapeseed oil or mild olive oil

½ cup packed light brown sugar

⅓ cup maple syrup

2 teaspoons kosher salt (Diamond Crystal or about half as much Morton)

½ cup golden raisins

¼ cup dried currants

Get your oven to 325°F. Line a baking sheet with parchment paper.

Spread the shredded coconut on the baking sheet and bake, rotating the pan halfway through, until light brown, 5 to 8 minutes. Dump the coconut into a small bowl and let it hang out.

Turn your oven temp to 275°F.

Mix together the oats and chopped mixed nuts in a large heatproof bowl. In a small pot, get the oil, brown sugar, maple syrup, and salt to a boil, stirring occasionally, then dump the mixture into the bowl. Mix it all real good to coat the oats and nuts.

On that same parchment paper–lined baking sheet, evenly spread the oat mixture into more or less a single layer and bake until the oats turn a nice caramel color, 2 to 2½ hours. Give it a little stir every 45 minutes or so, but if you like clusters, not so much near the end.

Take the mixture out of the oven and let it cool a bit. Add the toasted coconut, raisins, and currants and mix it all together. Let it cool completely, when it shall fulfill its crunchy promise.

Eat it now or keep it in an airtight container at room temp for up to 1 month.

LIZ'S CARROT MARMALADE

Liz Hollinger, pastry chef and co-leader of the kitchen at Molly's Rise and Shine, was the reason that we turned yogurt-for-breakfast into a carrot dish. She made this component based off a similar marmalade she tried in Greece. She killed it, and our carrot yogurt (see page 21) wouldn't be the same without it. Makes about 2 cups

1 tablespoon white sugar, plus 1⅓ cups

1½ teaspoons powdered fruit pectin

4 cups carrot juice (from the store)

2 cinnamon sticks

1 tablespoon plus 1 teaspoon pink peppercorns

6 whole cloves

6 cardamom pods, smashed open

Mix together the 1 tablespoon sugar and the pectin in a small bowl. That's your pectin bomb, and you're gonna need it toward the end.

Put everything else into a medium heavy pot and bring to a boil over high heat. Lower the heat and cook at a rolling simmer, stirring occasionally, until the liquid reduces by about half, 30 minutes or so.

Pour the mixture through a fine-mesh strainer, discard the solids, then return the liquid to the pot. Stir in the pectin bomb, get the mixture boiling again over high heat, then boil, stirring nonstop, until it looks glossy and thickens enough to easily coat the back of a spoon, about 2 minutes. Let it cool completely.

It keeps in the fridge for up to 1 month.

MOLLY'S BISCUITS

These are the best biscuits I've ever had, and I don't have shit to do with them. Credit goes to a slew of people, beginning with chef de cuisine Nate, who kicked off this triumphant year-long pursuit of deliciousness; he spent a solid six months experimenting before we opened our breakfast spot, Molly's, and stole his mom's boyfriend's move of adding white vinegar (to amp up buttermilk's tang). Swade gets some credit, too, for pissing in the punch bowl when he chimed in, *months* into Nate's struggle, with, "Why not try citric acid instead of vinegar?" Fucker was right.

But the lion's share goes to brilliant pastry chefs Liz and Jess, who gave the Biscuit Boys a good-job pat and then fixed our shit. They froze and grated the butter, which creates little pockets of steam in the oven and clinches a real tender crumb. They used two kinds of liquid fats: buttermilk for ooh-damn-tanginess and sour cream for richness. And they instituted some fold-and-roll action, giving it sandwich-friendly structure for, say, the breakfast sandwich of my dreams: scrambled eggs, Jimmy Dean, cheddar, and mayo. Or, just top with some Country Gravy Upgrade (page 28).

P.S. Citric acid is easy to buy online, at baking supply stores, and even at a lot of grocery stores.

MAKES 12

1½ sticks (12 tablespoons) unsalted butter, frozen

1½ cups buttermilk

½ cup plus 2 tablespoons sour cream

4 cups all-purpose flour, plus more for rolling

2 tablespoons plus 2¼ teaspoons baking powder

2 tablespoons kosher salt (Diamond Crystal or about half as much Morton)

1 tablespoon white sugar

1½ teaspoons citric acid (see P.S.)

1 egg

1 tablespoon heavy cream or whole milk

Flaky sea salt (optional)

Get your oven to 400°F. Line a large baking sheet with parchment paper (or lightly coat the baking sheet with nonstick spray).

Use the large holes of a box grater to grate the frozen butter into a bowl, then put it back in the freezer. In a medium mixing bowl, whisk together the buttermilk and sour cream and set aside in the fridge. In a large mixing bowl, whisk together the flour, baking powder, kosher salt, sugar, and citric acid.

Now, you want to make the dough without warming the butter too much. So get ready—speed is important from here on. Add the grated butter to the flour mixture and toss well with your hands, breaking up any big clumps of butter but not doing the usual "working in the butter" business. Instead, you're basically just coating the butter bits in the dry stuff.

Next, pour in the buttermilk mixture and use a flexible spatula to mix everything together in about eight big swooping folds. You're trying to get all of the dry mixture wet without working it too much (that'd give you chewy biscuits). Then, use your hands to quickly finish the dough, giving it a couple of folds in the bowl and incorporating any wet or dusty spots.

continued

Dust the counter with about ¼ cup all-purpose flour. Give yourself a good 2 feet by 1 foot of space for the biscuits, even though you're not going to roll them that big. Dump the dough onto the floured surface and dust the top of the dough blob with another 2 tablespoons or so flour. Pat the dough blob into a rough 6-inch square that's about 2 inches high.

Using a rolling pin and working from the middle out, roll out the dough to a nice even 10-inch square. Use your hands to brush off any excess flour.

Fold one of the sides about a third of the way over the dough, then fold the opposite side over the folded dough. Rotate the dough a quarter turn clockwise (or at least the same direction each time) and roll out the dough to make that nice even square again. Repeat this process (fold like a letter, quarter turn, and roll it out) three more times, for a total of four folds, but on the last time, stop before you roll it into the 10-inch square. If your square begins to look wonky, take a moment to pat the dough into a neater rectangle between those quarter turns.

After the fourth fold, roll out the dough once more, but this time make a rectangle measuring about 7 by 10 inches. Trim the edges with a bench scraper or knife—a straight edge makes the biscuits rise better. Cut the dough into twelve 2- to 2½-inch squares and put them on the baking sheet with a good 2 inches between each one.

In a small bowl, whisk together the egg and heavy cream until there are no blobs of egg whites. Brush or rub the biscuit tops with a thin layer of this egg business, then lightly sprinkle with flaky sea salt.

Bake on the center rack, rotating the pan halfway through, until the undersides are fully golden brown and a toothpick poked in the center comes out nice and dry, 20 minutes or so. Serve the biscuits warm.

Wrap up any leftovers. They'll stay pretty delicious in the fridge for a couple of days and freeze well, too. Reheat in a low oven before serving them again.

Mollys
Breakfast
Retreat

COUNTRY GRAVY UPGRADE

Colleen makes this mean sausage gravy for when biscuits (see page 25) need smothering. Pour it on, then add fresh cracked pepper for flavor and maybe some chopped scallion to ward off scurvy.

(see page 25)

MAKES ABOUT 5 CUPS

Get the bacon fat hot in a medium skillet over medium heat. Sprinkle in the flour and immediately get whisking and keep whisking until the resulting roux turns the sandy brown color of Brad Pitt's hair when it was long in the '90s, 3 to 5 minutes. Scrape the roux into a bowl and set aside.

Get a medium Dutch oven or heavy pot hot over medium-high heat, then add the sausage and brown, breaking up clumps and stirring sometimes, about 5 minutes. Scoop the sausage onto a plate, leaving any fat behind (if there's not much, add another teaspoon or two of bacon fat), then add the onions and garlic and sauté in the fat until the onions are translucent, 5 to 7 minutes. Add the roux, along with the miso, thyme, sage, and browned sausage and cook, stirring frequently, for a couple of minutes, so the flavors meld.

Stir in the milk, cream, hot sauce, vinegar, and Worcestershire sauce; and let it simmer; and cook, whisking sometimes, until it thickens (it should look like the gravy from Thanksgiving commercials), 5 to 10 minutes. Stir in the pepper and salt, and it's ready to pour over biscuits.

Fully cooled, it keeps in the fridge for up to 1 week. Reheat it gently with a splash of water or milk.

¼ cup rendered bacon fat, lard, or unsalted butter, plus a little more if needed

¼ cup all-purpose flour

12 ounces raw breakfast sausage (preferably Jimmy Dean)

2 large white or yellow onions, cut into small dice (about 4 cups)

¼ cup finely chopped garlic

1½ tablespoons awase miso

2 teaspoons chopped thyme

2 teaspoons finely chopped sage

4 cups whole milk

1 cup heavy cream

1 tablespoon Louisiana-style hot sauce

Scant 1 teaspoon apple cider vinegar

Scant 1 teaspoon Worcestershire sauce

1 tablespoon freshly ground black pepper

2 teaspoons kosher salt (Diamond Crystal or about half as much Morton)

GRAND SLAM McMUFFIN

This breakfast sandwich is as American as gluttony and cease-and-desist letters. After many overthought iterations, we settled on this version, which merges the simple joys of the Egg McMuffin with the bounty of a Denny's Grand Slam. Since Day One, we garnished it with a mini flag on a toothpick, with a brief hiatus when the country veered toward fucking Donald's alt-right autocracy.

Feel free to use your favorite local breakfast sausage instead of Jimmy Dean if you're OK trading a clear conscience for inferior flavor. Options for the hash browns include deep-frying them at home like an overachiever, or my favorite, buying them at a fast-food joint and booking it home in an attempt to serve them hot, then inevitably giving them a few minutes in the oven.

MAKES 4

1 tablespoon vegetable oil, plus more for deep-frying (about 2 quarts; optional but optimal)

Four ½-inch-thick round slices yellow or white onion

½ teaspoon kosher salt (Diamond Crystal or about half as much Morton), plus more if you like

4 frozen hash brown patties (if you didn't buy them hot)

2 tablespoons unsalted butter, room-temp so it's mayo-soft

4 English muffins, split

1 pound Jimmy Dean pork sausage, made into four ¼-inch-thick patties

4 slices American cheese

Ketchup (there is only Heinz) for serving

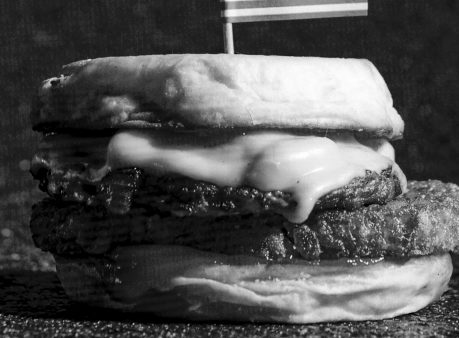

Pour the 1 tablespoon oil into a large nonstick or well-seasoned cast-iron skillet, add the onion slices in a single layer, and set the skillet over medium-high heat. Let the onions get a nice, even chocolate brown on the bottom, about 10 minutes, then flip them and do it again, 6 to 8 minutes more. Add the salt, stir to separate the rings, and cook for another minute or so to cook off any remaining rawness. Move the rings to a bowl or plate and set them aside.

Fry the hash browns according to the instructions on page 94. (If you bought them, stick them in a 400°F oven to warm them up.)

Put the skillet back over medium heat. Generously butter the cut sides of the English muffins, then add to the skillet, cut-side down and in batches, and brown, until they're a nice toasty color, 2 to 3 minutes. Set them aside.

In that same skillet, cook your sausage patties over medium-high heat until they are good and browned on the bottom, about 2 minutes. Flip them, then top them each with three or four onion rings and then a slice of cheese. Keep cooking until the sausage is cooked through and the cheese is fully melted, about 2 minutes more.

Hit both halves of the English muffins with a generous squirt of ketchup. Top the bottom halves with the hash browns, followed by the cheesy sausages, and top those with the rest of the English muffins. Get into it.

IN PRAISE OF JIM DEAN

I'm not sure if it's nostalgia, the spice extractives, or whatever industrial magic has to happen for the second ingredient on the packaging to be water, but for me, Jimmy Dean is king. To make sure people eat with their hearts and not their minds, I like to call it "sausage in the style of Jim Dean" so no one knows whether we made or bought it.

MEATLOAF: THE BAGEL, NOT THE MUSICIAN

When you see a dish and think, "Wow, how did the chef think to combine those flavors?" I like to think it's because they happened to be near each other in the kitchen. That's the reason we first tried peanut butter salsa macha with collards (see page 18) and hog's head cheese on tortillas. And that's how we formulated this banging bagel. The nice people at Black Seed Bagels in NYC had invited us to make a guest sandwich, and almost all the components were sitting on Colleen's station.

And if you think it's weird to slip melty cheese–covered meatloaf onto a bagel slathered with flavored cream cheese, well, you're probably right. It's pretty damn good, though.

MAKES 4

Eight ½-inch-thick slices meatloaf (see facing page)

8 slices American cheese

4 tablespoons unsalted butter, room-temp so it's mayo-soft

4 plain, garlic, or sesame bagels, halved

½ cup Pizza Cream Cheese (page 223), room-temp so it's nice and soft

Handful of basil leaves

Some thinly sliced red onion

Heaping ⅓ cup sliced hot pickled cherry peppers, or more if you like

Put a baking sheet in your oven and preheat it to 400°F. While it's heating up, grab a second baking sheet and arrange the meatloaf slices in overlapping pairs so they're about as wide as the bagels. Top each pair with two overlapping slices of cheese. Butter each bagel.

When the oven is preheated, put the bagels, cut-side down, on the hot baking sheet and add the other baking sheet with the meatloaf to the oven. Bake until the cheese has fully melted and the bagels are golden brown, 5 to 7 minutes.

To build each sandwich, liberally smear the cream cheese on the bottom bagel halves. Use a spatula to add the cheesy meatloaf slices, then top with the basil, onion, and cherry peppers. Add the bagel tops and eat.

TREATISE ON FROMAGE AMÉRICAIN

Not all American cheese (or "Pasteurized Process American cheese," as it's officially called) is the same. For instance, no hate for Kraft Singles and other individually wrapped slices of American over by the milk at the grocery store, but they just don't have the flavor of the stuff you find in the deli section. Meltability is another important factor. Only the world's greatest scientists know why some American cheese refuses to melt, but it's true and it sucks. The good news is plenty of widely available brands have the meltability you're after, but you have to find them. To guide your search, I've found that the brands with the word "deli" in the title are the way to go. Once you've found your baby, hold it tight.

MEATLOAF: THE MEATLOAF, NOT THE MUSICIAN

This meatloaf is easy and I love it. I don't put tiny little vegetable pieces in my meatloaf because that shit is weird. It also takes extra work, and this meatloaf is made for sandwiches (see facing page and page 129), so I doubt anyone would detect the tiny little vegetables anyway. Also, you'll notice there's no glaze—again, sandwiches—though, for the record, this would probably be pretty delicious if you glazed it. So to eat it as a standalone dish, maybe Google "meatloaf glaze" and follow that recipe, unless it sounds gross. **Serves 6 for dinner (makes 12 sandwich slices)**

Get your oven to 350°F.

Combine the eggs, ketchup, sour cream, Worcestershire sauce, mustard, rosemary, salt, chili powder, garlic powder, onion powder, and paprika in your blender and buzz on high speed until smooth, about 1 minute. Dump the blender contents into a large mixing bowl, add the ground beef and crackers, and use your hands to mix it all up, so everything's well distributed.

Line a loaf pan with parchment paper so the paper hangs over the sides by an inch or two. Transfer the mixture to the pan and pat the top so it's nice and even. Bake, uncovered, until it's cooked through (peek in the center with a knife or go with 155°F on a meat thermometer), 45 to 50 minutes. Let the meatloaf rest for 15 minutes or so.

To eat it hot, go ahead and slice it up. It might fall apart, but who cares.

To make neat slices for sandwiches, let it cool completely in the pan, about 1 hour. Refrigerate for up to 4 days, then slice it when you're ready to go.

2 eggs

¾ cup ketchup (there is only Heinz)

¼ cup sour cream

3 tablespoons Worcestershire sauce

2 tablespoons Dijon mustard

2 tablespoons roughly chopped rosemary leaves

1 tablespoon plus 2 teaspoons kosher salt (Diamond Crystal or about half as much Morton)

1 tablespoon chili powder

1 tablespoon garlic powder

1 tablespoon onion powder

1 tablespoon smoked paprika

2 pounds ground beef

35 saltine crackers, buzzed to fine bread crumb–size (about 1 cup)

THE SALAD R

BRUNCH 2

Salad

BUFFALO WALDORF SALAD

I've been making this one for years, back when I was cooking food that didn't come on garage-sale McDonald's plates and did catering for movie productions and once saw Tom Cruise walking. It came from some of my favorite foods playing a game of telephone in my head after a couple of tokes.

The celery in the classic Waldorf got me thinking about blue cheese and Buffalo wings, and next thing you know I'm frying apples and reducing hot sauce, then mounting it with butter. And that's how we made wing sauce at Turkey and the Wolf. That is until one day in a pinch, Nate swapped in Frank's RedHot wing sauce and called to inform me we that didn't have to worry about making our own no more. And I said, That's good. One less thing.

To pickle the celery: Put the celery in a small heatproof bowl. In a small pot, bring the rice vinegar, sugar, salt, and ⅓ cup water to a boil, stirring so the sugar dissolves. Pour the boiling liquid over the celery, give it a stir, and let it cool to room temperature. It's good to go and keeps in the fridge for up to 1 month.

To make the dish: Set up a cooling rack or line a baking sheet with paper towels. Get 2 inches of oil to 350°F in a heavy pot over medium-high heat. While it's heating up, combine the sugar and salt in a small bowl. In a medium bowl, combine the seltzer and flour and gently whisk it together until it's smooth. Pop this batter in the fridge until the oil's ready.

When you're ready to fry, core the apples, then slice them into half-moons that are somewhere between ⅛ and ¼ inch thick.

Working in four batches, dip the apple slices, one by one, in the batter, then carefully add them to the oil. Fry, flipping them once with tongs halfway through and trying your best to separate any that stick together, until they're light golden brown, 5 to 6 minutes per batch. Move them to the cooling rack or prepared baking sheet and season with the sugar-salt mixture, then repeat with the rest of the batches.

Once the apples are all fried and seasoned up, move them to a platter. Spoon the Frank's over them and top with the candied walnuts, blue cheese, pickled celery (but not the liquid), and scallions. Grind on some pepper and serve with the bottle of Frank's on the table for anyone who's feeling extra spicy.

SERVES 2 TO 4

Pickled Celery

3 large celery stalks, very thinly sliced on the diagonal

⅓ cup unseasoned rice vinegar

⅓ cup white sugar

1 teaspoon kosher salt (Diamond Crystal or about half as much Morton)

For the Dish

Vegetable oil for deep-frying (about 2 quarts)

1½ teaspoons white sugar

1½ teaspoons kosher salt (Diamond Crystal or about half as much Morton)

1 cup very cold seltzer

¾ cup all-purpose flour

2 large medium-tart apples, like Pink Lady or Honeycrisp

¼ cup Frank's RedHot Buffalo Wings Sauce, plus more for serving

1 cup Candied Walnuts (page 40), roughly chopped

½ cup crumbled blue cheese

2 scallions, very thinly sliced (on the diagonal, for the 'gram)

Freshly ground black pepper

CANDIED WALNUTS

I like these because they're easy to make, they come out nice and glassy, and they're not mega sweet. As my wife, Lauren, put it: Less candy, more crunch. Makes 2 cups

2 cups raw walnuts

1 cup light corn syrup

1 cup white sugar

½ teaspoon kosher salt (Diamond Crystal or about half as much Morton)

Get your oven to 350°F and line a baking sheet with parchment paper (for easy cleanup). Lightly coat the paper with nonstick spray, if you've got some, to make your life a little easier after cooking.

Combine the walnuts, corn syrup, sugar, and 1 cup water in a medium pot, set it over high heat, and bring to a boil. Turn down the heat and cook at a pretty active simmer until the simmer-bubbles get big (a few should be about an inch wide), 15 to 20 minutes. Immediately strain the walnuts, discarding the syrupy liquid and tossing the walnuts a bit to drain off any excess. Transfer the walnuts to the baking sheet, sprinkle the salt on top, and bake them in the oven until they turn a nice copper brown, 15 to 20 minutes. Remove from the oven.

When the walnuts are cool enough to handle, transfer them to a storage container. If you didn't use nonstick spray, just get in there with a thin spatula to help them release from the parchment.

These guys can be stored at room temp for up to 1 week.

HOW TO DEEP-FRY YOUR FEELINGS

You can bake my chicken potpies (see page 133) in the oven. You can and probably should grab hash browns at a drive-thru. But a handful of recipes in this book require deep-frying, like the chicken fried steak (see page 109), apple fritters (see page 171), and Buffalo Waldorf Salad (page 39). I'm here to show you that deep-frying is fun, and you can do it! All you need is a little equipment, a few tips, and the knowledge that you're beautiful and you're worth it.

Here's what you need:

- a shit ton of oil

- a nice, tall heavy pot

- a candy or deep-fry thermometer

- a mesh strainer, kitchen spider, or some tongs

Two inches of oil is reasonable for frying at home. In a medium pot, that's about 2 quarts.

Clip that candy or deep-fry thermometer onto the pot. It lets you take the temp of the oil and monitor as you fry, so you can adjust the heat underneath accordingly. As the oil's coming up, give it an occasional stir so you don't have hot or cold spots.

Fry in batches to avoid crowding the oil. Otherwise, the oil temp will drop too much and you end up with an oily, soggy product.

Once things are crispy, use the strainer, spider, or tongs to move the fried goodies to a tray or plate lined with paper towels, to slurp up any excess oil. If the recipe calls for salting or sprinkling on stuff after frying, do that right away, so the seasonings grab on.

THE CABBAGE PATCH

A mashup of two of my favorite salads ever: We take the refreshing cabbage-and-herb combo from Vietnamese classic ga xe phay and toss it with the spicy, lime-y coconut milk dressing from NYC restaurant Uncle Boon's (RIP). Uncle Boon's was one of the coolest places on Earth, and Ann Redding and Matt Danzer, the geniuses there, used it for their banana blossom salad. The dressing is so good that I could eat it like soup, which means the salad is impossible to overdress. We also toss on some roasted, salted sunflower seeds, which is one of my go-to moves for taking salads to crunchy town.

SERVES 6 TO 8

8 cups very, very thinly sliced green cabbage (1 small head)

1 small red onion, sliced into thin half-moons

1 cup roughly chopped cilantro

1 cup Thai basil leaves, roughly chopped

¼ cup fresh lime juice (from 2 to 3 limes)

2 tablespoons thinly sliced lemongrass (tender insides only), from 1 large stalk

1 jalapeño, very thinly sliced

Heaping 1 cup Pig Ear Cracklins Upgrade (page 45)

1½ cups Coconut-Chile Dressing (page 44)

Kosher salt (optional)

½ cup roasted salted hulled sunflower seeds

½ cup Thai or Vietnamese fried garlic

In a large mixing bowl, toss together the cabbage, onion, cilantro, basil, lime juice, lemongrass, jalapeño, and cracklins, breaking the cracklins up a bit if they've clumped while frying. Add the dressing, toss really well, then taste and add some salt, if you want.

Put it in a serving bowl or on a platter, sprinkle with the sunflower seeds and fried garlic, and eat up.

COCONUT-CHILE DRESSING

This superb balancing act of a dressing is based on the wildly delicious one from what *was* probably my favorite restaurant: Uncle Boon's in NYC. It's closed now, but chefs Matt Danzer and Ann Redding used the expertly calibrated pungent mixture—spicy and sweet, tart and salty, plus a dose of coconut milk to tame the intensity—to electrify a Thai-style salad made with shredded banana blossom and rotisserie chicken. Our version of their triumph goes on shredded cabbage, but you can use it on a ton of stuff. **Makes about 1½ cups**

Get the oil shimmering in a small pot over medium heat. Cook the onion, garlic, Thai chiles, and galangal in there until they all soften a bit, about 5 minutes. Add the fish sauce, sugar, shrimp paste, chile flakes, sriracha, and tamarind concentrate and cook, stirring often, until the onion is fully soft, about 10 minutes. Take it off the heat.

Stir in the coconut milk and lime juice, then pour it into your blender and blend until smooth. Let it cool fully.

It keeps in an airtight container in the fridge for up to 10 days.

2 tablespoons vegetable oil

1 small white onion, cut into ¼-inch pieces

3 garlic cloves, roughly chopped

2 dried Thai chiles or other dried Asian red chiles, stemmed

One ½-inch piece fresh or thawed frozen galangal, peeled and finely chopped

1 tablespoon fish sauce

1 tablespoon white sugar

2 teaspoons Thai shrimp paste

2 teaspoons gochugaru (Korean chile flakes) or other red chile flakes

1 teaspoon Huy Fong Foods Sriracha

1 teaspoon jarred tamarind concentrate

1 cup unsweetened coconut milk

2 tablespoons fresh lime juice

I LOVE GOCHUGARU

I love the gentle heat and complexity (fruity, slightly smoky) of gochugaru, so it's indispensable in my pantry. Look for the coarse flakes at Korean supermarkets or order them online. If you have flavorful, coarsely ground dried chile, like Aleppo, in your pantry, it'll work for my recipes. And if I'm honest, so will generic red chile flakes.

PIG EAR CRACKLINS UPGRADE

These are awesome but optional in the Cabbage Patch salad (page 42), and they're super-snackable on their own. Since they're nice when warm, in the same way tortilla chips are, you can enjoy them hot out of the fryer or stick them in a hot oven for a few minutes before digging in.

MAKES ABOUT 3 CUPS

2 or 3 pig ears (about 12 ounces total)

Vegetable oil or canola oil for deep-frying (about 2 quarts)

1 teaspoon kosher salt (Diamond Crystal or about half as much Morton)

Put the ears in a big pot, cover them with a good 6 inches of water (if they float, use a spider, skimmer, or strainer to weigh them down) and bring the water to a boil. Cook at a steady simmer (topping it off with hot water, if necessary, so the ears stay submerged) until they're so tender that they tear easily, 3 to 4 hours.

Drain them, let cool completely, and then slice them into long strips that are about ⅛ inch thick. They'll keep in the fridge for up to 4 days or in the freezer for up to 6 months.

Line a large mixing bowl with paper towels. Pat the pig-ear strips dry.

Get 2 inches of oil to 350°F in a really deep, heavy pot over medium-high heat. (You want it deep to keep the inevitable splatter from coming for you. If you don't have a super-deep pot, consider working in smaller batches—and hold on to your butt.)

Use a long-handled skimmer to carefully add the pig-ear strips to the oil (stand back, because they'll crackle and pop like crazy) and cover with a splatter screen, if you've got one. Cook, carefully stirring after a minute or so to keep them from clumping too much, until they're golden brown and they stop bubbling, 3 to 5 minutes. Use the skimmer to move them to the mixing bowl, immediately sprinkle on the salt, and toss well. They're good to go.

Cooled completely, they keep in an airtight container at room temp for up to 3 days.

LEFTOVER FRIED CHICKEN SALAD

My dad had cold fried chicken in his fridge at all times—also, Diet Coke and at least two things of Ben and Jerry's with about half a bite left in them, which I've never really understood. The cold fried chicken, though, I get. It's great for snacking, obviously, but you could also make this dish, a Day One item at Turkey and the Wolf, that we made with fried smoked bird. It's bright and refreshing thanks to herbs, lemon, and crisp veggie stuff—or, at least, refreshing for a salad of fried chicken dressed with mayo and sour cream. Definitely do not smoke and fry any birds. Use regular fried chicken leftovers or get a spicy four-piece at Popeyes.

Gently simmer the sweet potato in slightly salty water just until cooked through, 15 to 20 minutes.

Meanwhile, combine the mayo, sour cream, mustard, hot sauce, pickles, celery, onion, dill, pepper, and the juice of half a lemon in a medium bowl and stir well to make a dressing.

When the sweet potato is done, drain well and spread out on a large plate or baking sheet to cool completely. Combine the sweet potato, fried chicken, and dressing in a large serving bowl and mix well. If it needs some, add salt and more pepper and lemon juice. Sprinkle with the scallions and some dill. Serve right away.

SERVES 4 TO 6

1 large sweet potato (about 1¼ pounds), peeled and cut into 1-inch cubes

⅓ cup mayo (Duke's or bust)

⅓ cup sour cream

3 tablespoons Creole mustard (like Zatarain's), or whole-grain mustard

2 tablespoons Louisiana-style hot sauce

¼ cup finely chopped bread-and-butter pickles

¼ cup finely chopped celery

¼ cup finely chopped red onion

1 tablespoon finely chopped dill, plus more for garnish

1 teaspoon freshly ground black pepper, or more if you like

½ juicy lemon, or more if you like

4 pieces leftover fried chicken, pulled off the bone into bite-size pieces (about 3 cups)

Kosher salt

2 tablespoons thinly sliced scallions

SUNDAY MORNING COMING-DOWN POTATO SALAD

Many (long, drunken, merry) Saturdays in Louisiana begin with a seafood boil, where giant pots of seafood, potatoes, and other stuff is turned out on a newspaper-lined picnic table and everyone goes at it with their hands. If there's anything left over, I'll make this spicy potato salad the following morning. Sunday—in the style of Kris Kristofferson, who, by the way, looks like my dad (check out the portrait on page 185)—is a hell of a lot easier with this calling your name.

There's no need to make a proper boil to re-create the magic, which, if you ask me, is the potatoes that have slurped up the salty, spicy, lemony liquid. Crab is great in there and, for most of you, easier to get than crawfish. Shrimp work, too. Just give them a quick poach in the potato cooking liquid.

SERVES 4 TO 6

Potatoes

1 pound red potatoes, halved

¼ cup powdered crab boil spice (like Zatarain's)

¼ cup powdered Zatarain's Pro Boil, or another ¼ cup crab boil spice

2 tablespoons Louisiana-style hot sauce

1 tablespoon kosher salt (Diamond Crystal or about half as much Morton)

1 tablespoon hondashi (bonito soup stock base), or another 1½ teaspoons kosher salt

3 juicy lemons, halved

For the Dish

10 Keebler Club Original Crackers

1½ teaspoons Old Bay Seasoning

1 pound (about 2 cups) jumbo lump crabmeat, claw meat, or a mixture

2 cups shrettuce (see page 229)

¾ cup Big Zesty Buttermilk Dressing (page 226)

3 scallions, trimmed and thinly sliced

2 celery stalks, thinly sliced

2 juicy lemons, halved

Kosher salt

To make the potatoes: Combine the potatoes, crab boil spice, pro boil, hot sauce, salt, hondashi, and 8 cups cold water in a large pot. Squeeze the lemons into the pot, then add the spent halves. Bring to a boil, then turn down the heat to simmer gently until the potatoes are tender all the way through, 20 to 30 minutes. If they get a little too soft, no big deal.

Drain the potatoes, discarding the lemons but reserving the liquid for another round if you want. Let the potatoes cool until you can handle them, then cut them into about ½-inch pieces.

To assemble the dish: Combine the crackers and Old Bay in a small resealable bag, seal it, and smash the crackers into pebbly pieces. Get into it—this is fun. Set them aside.

In a large mixing bowl, combine the boiled potatoes, crabmeat, shrettuce, dressing, scallions, and celery, then squeeze on about ¼ cup lemon juice. Toss gently but really well so it's all coated with the dressing. Give it a taste and add salt and more lemon juice until you're happy. Sprinkle on as much of those crackers as you want.

Eat it.

THE WEDGE

Excess is the key to this salad. A borderline inappropriate amount of blue cheese dressing. Way more of that everything-bagel crunchy stuff than you think is reasonable. As much bacon as a salad can handle. And a heap of fresh dill. At Turkey and the Wolf, we use a half a head of iceberg doused in nearly a pint of dressing. At home, it's up to you.

To make the everything-bagel stuff: Put the sesame seeds, poppy seeds, dried minced garlic, and dried minced onion in a large heavy skillet; set it over medium-high heat; and stir and toss constantly until it all smells sweet and nutty, like a bagel shop, 3 to 5 minutes. Dump it all onto a plate or tray and spread it out so it cools quickly.

To assemble the salad: Line a plate with paper towels. Put the bacon in the skillet, set it over medium heat, and cook, stirring occasionally, until golden brown and almost crispy, about 10 minutes. Use a slotted spoon to scoop the bacon onto the plate. (Reserve the fat to make sausage gravy, see page 28, or because it's generally great to cook with.)

Whack the lettuce heads stem-side down on the counter, which makes it easier to remove the bottom nubs. Or just cut the stems off. Ditch any bruised outer leaves. Cut each head in half or into equal-size wedges (whichever you want). Put the pieces on a platter, sprinkle a pinch of salt and pepper on each one, then pour on the dressing and sprinkle on an offensive amount of the everything-bagel stuff.

In a small mixing bowl, gently toss the cherry tomatoes with the oil, a generous squeeze of lemon juice, and a generous pinch of salt and pepper. Garnish the salad with the tomatoes, dill, and bacon. Some more pepper is good here, too.

SERVES 6 TO 8

Everything-Bagel Stuff

¼ cup sesame seeds

¼ cup poppy seeds

¼ cup dried minced garlic

¼ cup dried minced onion

Salad

1 pound slab bacon, cut into ½-inch pieces

2 heads iceberg lettuce

Kosher salt

Coarsely cracked black pepper

2 cups Chunky Blue Cheese Dressing (page 54)

2 cups cherry tomatoes, halved

Splash of extra-virgin olive oil

½ juicy lemon

Small handful of tender sprigs dill, torn

CHUNKY BLUE CHEESE DRESSING

This one's all Colleen Quarls. The original chef de cuisine at Turkey and the Wolf—and now running things at our breakfast spot, Molly's Rise and Shine—Colleen took all of five minutes to make blue cheese dressing that was just the right amount of tangy from buttermilk and lemon; just the right amount of ranch-y from garlic, onion, and celery; and awesomely sharp and funky from blue cheese. She's that good. **Makes about 3 cups**

10 ounces blue cheese, crumbled (about 1¼ cups)

1 cup mayo (Duke's or bust)

½ cup sour cream

¼ cup buttermilk

1 tablespoon fresh lemon juice, or more if you like

1 tablespoon poppy seeds

1½ teaspoons Louisiana-style hot sauce

1½ teaspoons garlic powder

1¼ teaspoons onion powder

1 teaspoon freshly ground black pepper

½ teaspoon celery salt

½ teaspoon celery seed

Kosher salt

In a medium bowl, mix together the blue cheese, mayo, sour cream, buttermilk, lemon juice, poppy seeds, hot sauce, garlic powder, onion powder, pepper, celery salt, and celery seed. If you want, add some salt and more lemon juice until you're happy.

It keeps in an airtight container in the fridge for up to 1 week.

LAMB, PEAS, MINT, AND CEREAL SALAD

Here's one I make at home. The base is a room-temp ground meat situation that will be vaguely familiar to lovers of northeastern Thai–style larb, and the crispy rice and sweet-sour-salty dressing make me think of the absolutely delightful Thai salad called yam khao tod. Because I decided to put lamb in there, I couldn't help but throw peas in, too, to complete the lamb, peas, and mint trifecta.

To make over those peas: An hour or so before serving, mix the salt and white sugar in a medium mixing bowl, then add the peas and stir well. Let them hang, then drain off any liquid that collects in the bowl. Taste them and, if they're a little too salty, give them a brief rinse under water.

To make the dressing: Buzz all the dressing ingredients in your blender until smooth with tiny specks of cilantro, about 1 minute. It tastes best day-of but will keep for a few days in the fridge.

To assemble the salad: Get a large skillet hot over medium heat. Add the Rice Krispies and cook, shaking and tossing often, until a good half of them turn liquor-store-bag brown and the others have darkened a shade or two, 1 to 2 minutes. Dump them onto a plate and set aside.

In that same skillet over medium heat, combine the oil and lamb and cook, stirring and breaking up clumps, for a few minutes. Stir in the sambal oelek, then keep cooking until the lamb is cooked through (i.e., no pink spots), 3 to 5 minutes more. Turn off the heat and let it cool slightly.

Scrape the lamb into a big mixing bowl, add the peas, peanuts, mint, and shallots, and give it all a good mix. Add half the dressing, then mix again until everything is dressed and hanging like buds. Then add more dressing to taste—I usually end up using all the dressing but it's a salty flavor bomb and I'm a freak. Sprinkle on the Rice Krispies and eat immediately.

SERVES 6 TO 8

Pea Makeover

1 tablespoon kosher salt (Diamond Crystal or about half as much Morton)

1½ teaspoons white sugar

3 cups (16-ounce bag) frozen peas, thawed and given a makeover (see page 73)

Dressing

⅔ cup fresh lime juice (from 5 to 7 limes)

½ cup fish sauce

½ cup roughly chopped cilantro

2 tablespoons packed light brown sugar

2 garlic cloves, peeled

2 tablespoons red chile flakes

2 tablespoons grapeseed oil or mild olive oil

Salad

2 cups Rice Krispies or another crisp rice cereal

2 teaspoons grapeseed oil or mild olive oil

1 pound ground lamb

2 tablespoons sambal oelek or sriracha

2 cups salted roasted peanuts

1 cup packed mint leaves, torn at the last minute

2 shallots, thinly sliced

BIG HAT, NO CATTLE

vegetables

3

SWEET POTATO BURRITO

We were twenty-four hours away from opening Turkey and the Wolf and there was still one sandwich we hadn't figured out. "Don't worry," I'd been telling my entire opening team, also known as Swade and Colleen, for days. "I got this." I did not have this.

My concept was for a sandwich with roasted sweet potatoes, whipped feta, and black garlic, which was so obviously going to be awesome. It was crap. After day two of watching me tinker desperately, Colleen stepped in. She suggested sweet potato fries, then we all got to riffing, and suddenly we had an actually great sandwich that was truly a team effort, like all our best food. Once we opened Molly's, the sandwich morphed into this breakfast burrito with the bizarrely harmonious medley of cream cheese, honey, jalapeños, and bread-and-butter pickles.

MAKES 4

Scallion Cream Cheese

1 cup (8 ounces) Philadelphia cream cheese, room-temp so it's nice and soft

1 scallion, trimmed and thinly sliced

¼ teaspoon kosher salt (Diamond Crystal or about half as much Morton)

Fries

Vegetable oil for deep-frying (about 2 quarts)

One 20-ounce bag frozen sweet potato waffle fries

1 teaspoon kosher salt (Diamond Crystal or about half as much Morton)

Burritos

4 tablespoons unsalted butter, room-temp so it's mayo-soft

Four 10-inch flour tortillas

Some thinly sliced red onion

24 bread-and-butter pickle chips

Heaping 2 cups packed arugula

1 or 2 small jalapeños, very thinly sliced

¼ cup honey (good and local, if possible)

To make the scallion cream cheese: Stir together the cream cheese, scallions, and salt in a medium bowl until well mixed. Set it aside. You can fridge it, too; just take it out 30 minutes before you eat so it can soften up again.

To make the fries: Get 2 inches of oil to 350°F. In batches, add the waffle fries and cook, occasionally stirring so they don't stick together, until they're hot and crispy, 3 to 5 minutes per batch. While you're frying, get your oven to 250°F and line a baking sheet with paper towels.

As the fries are done, use a spider or strainer to move them to the prepared baking sheet and sprinkle liberally with salt. Keep them warm in the oven (without the paper towel, if that concerns you).

To assemble the burritos: Make and serve one burrito at a time for max deliciousness. Set a large heavy skillet over medium heat until it's good and hot. Evenly swipe a thin layer of butter on both sides of a tortilla, then cook in the skillet so you get some nice brown spots on each side but it's still soft, 30 seconds or so per side.

Put the hot tortilla on a plate and apply a scant ¼ cup of the scallion cream cheese down the center of the tortilla in an even 2- or 3-inch-wide schmear. On the cream cheese, distribute a fourth of so of the onion, pickles, and arugula, plus as much jalapeño as you like. Pile on a fourth of the waffle fries and drizzle on 1 tablespoon honey.

Roll that sucker up nice and tight, so the ingredients get a bit scrunched. Serve it right away, then get to making the next ones.

ROASTED SUNCHOKE AND WHITE TRUFFLE DUNKAROOS

Sunchokes and truffles go together like rollerblading and Capri Sun—there's no better pairing. The knobby tubers get nutty and sweet when they're roasted and they taste real nice with white truffle, which hits you in a nice-stinky-cheese sorta way. Fresh white truffles are hilariously expensive, truffle oil is weird, but this pate stuff is awesome and worth the hit on your wallet.

I like to rewarm leftovers and mash the sunchokes to serve on toast slathered with the dip. The dip itself is also great with other roasted root vegetables and it's dope on steak.

Some people peel their sunchokes. I don't, because I like the slight chew of the skin, they look cooler unpeeled, and peeling those knobby bastards is annoying. Some people, it's recently come to my attention, call them fartichokes. If they mess with your business, you can totally sub in celery root or potatoes, at the risk of being basic.

SERVES 4 TO 6

Sunchokes

2 pounds sunchokes, scrubbed

1 tablespoon kosher salt (Diamond Crystal or about half as much Morton)

2 tablespoons extra-virgin olive oil

Dip

12 ounces (1½ cups) Philadelphia cream cheese, room-temp so it's nice and soft

3 tablespoons La Rustichella white truffle pate

1½ teaspoons kosher salt (Diamond Crystal or about half as much Morton), or more if you like

1½ teaspoons freshly ground black pepper

½ juicy lemon, or more if you like

To roast the chokes: Get your oven to 400°F.

While it's heating up, cut the sunchokes lengthwise in half (or if they're really big, slice them lengthwise into about ½-inch-thick slices). Toss them with the salt and olive oil in a medium bowl.

When the oven's preheated, scatter the sunchokes in a single layer onto one or two large baking sheets, cut-side down. Roast until brown and tender, not unlike a roasted chunk of potato, about 30 minutes.

To make the dip: Meanwhile, buzz the cream cheese, truffle pate, salt, pepper, and about 1½ tablespoons lemon juice in a food processor, occasionally stopping to swipe the sides with a rubber spatula and pulsing to break up the cream cheese blobs, until it's totally smooth, about 2 minutes. Season with more lemon juice and salt until you're happy.

Serve the hot sunchokes with a bowl of the truffle stuff for dunking.

WHITE BEAN HUMMUS WITH CHILE-CRUNCH PEAS

Like just about every chef I know who doesn't actually know shit about hummus, I look to my buddy Michael Solomonov for guidance. (His cookbooks are hot fire, so check them out!) If you love this dish like I do, you have him to thank, though if you don't, you have me to blame. I mean, I'm the one who decided to use white beans and mayo (which adds some je ne sais quoi creaminess and is also comically on-brand) and top it with peas and peanuts tossed with Chinese chile crisp.

Serve it with any dippables—raw vegetables, chips (tortilla, bagel, pita), or butter-toasted roti paratha (see page 135).

To make the chile-crunch peas: Stir together the salt and sugar in a small mixing bowl, then add the peas and mix well. Let it hang out for 1 hour, then drain off any liquid that collects in the bowl. Taste, and if they're a little too salty for your taste, give them a brief rinse under water.

Combine the peas, peanuts, and chile crisp in a medium mixing bowl and stir well. It keeps for up to 2 days in the fridge.

To make the hummus: Combine the garlic and salt in a food processor, squeeze in a good ⅓ cup lemon juice, and buzz until the garlic looks minced, about 30 seconds. Move it all to a small bowl and let it sit for 10 minutes to tone down the flavor of the garlic.

Set a fine-mesh strainer over the food processor, pour in the garlic mixture, and stir and press with a spoon or flexible spatula to extract as much liquid as you can. Discard the solids. Add the beans, tahini, oil, mayo, cumin, and 3 tablespoons cold water, then buzz until it's completely smooth, 1 to 2 minutes. Season with more salt and lemon juice until you're happy. It'll keep in the fridge for up to 5 days.

Serve the hummus in shallow bowls, top with the chile-crunch peas, and squeeze on a little more lemon juice for an extra pop of acidity.

SERVES 4 TO 6

Chile-Crunch Peas

1 teaspoon kosher salt (Diamond Crystal or about half as much Morton)

½ teaspoon white sugar

1 cup frozen peas, thawed

¼ cup salted, roasted peanuts, roughly chopped

2 tablespoons stirred-up Chinese chile crisp

Hummus

4 garlic cloves, unpeeled

2 teaspoons kosher salt (Diamond Crystal or about half as much Morton), or more if you like

3 juicy lemons, halved, or more if you like, plus another ½ juicy lemon

1¾ cups (19-ounce can) drained cannellini beans, rinsed under cold water

⅔ cup well-stirred high-quality tahini, like the Soom brand

3 tablespoons extra-virgin olive oil

1 tablespoon mayo (Duke's or bust)

½ teaspoon ground cumin

GAS-STATION TOSTADAS

If I had a dime for every meal I pieced together from the aisles of a gas station, I'd have a pool by now, or at least a hot tub. Both this tostada and its more sophisticated cousin, the Double-Decker Boomtown Upgrade (page 68), remind me of my favorite parts of those meals—that chip-level crunch, the umami blast of pop-top dips and bagged snacks.

The finishing touch is Dorito Dust, which was a gimmick in theory but stuck because it's awesome, a calibrated crumble of Nacho Cheese and Cool Ranch contributing just the right kind of salty, MSG-y *garniture*. We always take the flavor combinations at Turkey and the Wolf seriously, even if it's kinda silly and we are kinda inebriated.

Assemble each one yourself for a touch of class or put out the fixings and let everyone get involved.

Swipe a nice even layer of onion dip on each tostada (about 3 tablespoons), then sprinkle on the Dorito dust, scallions, and some pepper. Generously squeeze on some lemon juice and get at it.

MAKES 8

1½ cups My Best Try at Colleen's Onion Dip (page 228)

8 store-bought tostadas

Dorito Dust (page 68) for sprinkling

4 scallions, trimmed and thinly sliced

Freshly ground black pepper

1 juicy lemon, or more if you like

DOUBLE-DECKER BOOMTOWN UPGRADE

Take the gas-station tostada to the next level by welcoming another crispy tortilla slathered with more awesome stuff to the party. It's the type of celebration where you eat all the seven-layer dip and don't wait 30 minutes before getting in the pool.

MAKES 4

¾ cup Gas-Station Bean Dip (page 227)

8 store-bought tostadas

¾ cup My Best Try at Colleen's Onion Dip (page 228)

½ cup coarsely grated sharp cheddar

Heaping ½ cup shrettuce (see page 229)

Dorito Dust (recipe follows) for sprinkling

⅔ cup sliced canned black olives

Freshly ground black pepper

1 juicy lemon, or more if you like

Take the bean dip out of the fridge 10 to 15 minutes before you want to eat, so it softens up a bit for spreading. Swipe a nice even layer of bean dip (about 3 tablespoons) on four of the tostadas, and swipe the onion dip (same) on the other four.

Divide the cheese and shrettuce among the four bean dip–slathered tostadas, then top them with the onion dip tostadas. Sprinkle on the Dorito dust, olives, and some pepper. Generously squeeze on some lemon juice and get at it.

DORITO DUST

This is a productive, and also ridiculous, way to spend a few minutes. If you're going to do it, though, do it right, take the extra step, and count out those chips, because reaching that Nacho Cheese–to–Cool Ranch sweet spot is pivotal. I use a mortar and pestle made from igneous rock forged in the furnace of an active volcano to crush them, but seeing as you're just taking Doritos and making them smaller, feel free to choose your own adventure.

The generosity with which you sprinkle this stuff on Gas-Station Tostadas (page 67) is proportional to your affection for marijuana, so scale up the recipe accordingly. **Makes about ¾ cup**

One 2.75-ounce bag Nacho Cheese Doritos (or 20 chips)

Half a 2.75-ounce bag Cool Ranch Doritos (or 10 chips)

Pound, grind, or crush all the Doritos to a coarse "dust" about the consistency of raw grits.

It keeps in a bag with a chip clip for as long as Doritos do, which is a long-ass while.

VISUALIZE WHIRLED PEAS ON TOAST

SERVES 4 TO 8

Some cooks look to the seasons or great chefs for inspiration. We look to bad puns. Whirled peas, a dish named long before it was created, was a no-brainer, and we visualized it as some peas whirled in a food processor with herby sauce. It's on toast, because I'm real big on eating food on toast. And it's got feta cream cheese because I'm real big on cream cheese. The lemon and herbs are clutch. A little too much is exactly the right amount.

To whirl those peas: Combine the peas and blender sauce in a food processor and pulse about ten times, just to mix the ingredients and chop the peas a bit, so there aren't any whole peas hanging around.

To make those toasts: Get a well-seasoned cast-iron skillet or griddle hot over medium heat. Swipe the butter on each side of the bread and toast in batches in the skillet until both sides are golden brown, 1 to 2 minutes per side. When they're done, move them to a rack or stand them up so they lean against each other, to keep from getting soggy.

When the bread is cool enough to handle, swipe each slice with the cream cheese, then cut the toasts in half—I'm a triangle guy, so I do corner to corner.

Spoon on all of the whirled peas (it'll only seem like too much until you taste it), then sprinkle on the onion, herbs, and almonds. Finally, squeeze on the juice from about half the lemon if it's super-juicy, or more if it's not.

Eat it.

Whirled Peas

3 cups (16-ounce bag) frozen peas, thawed, or even better, given a makeover (see page 73)

½ cup Verdant Blender Sauce (page 216)

Toasts

3 tablespoons unsalted butter, room-temp so it's mayo-soft

4 thick slices soft white bread

½ cup Feta Cream Cheese (page 72), room-temp so it's nice and soft

Some thinly sliced white or yellow onion

¼ cup packed picked dill sprigs

¼ cup packed mint leaves, torn if large

Heaping ¼ cup toasted slivered almonds or chopped roasted almonds

1 juicy lemon

FETA CREAM CHEESE

And like magic, you can turn your feta into creamy feta. Put this on a sandwich, try it with whirled peas (see page 71), or throw on some herbs and use it as a dip. Makes about 1½ cups

1 cup (5 ounces) crumbled feta

¼ teaspoon kosher salt (Diamond Crystal or about half as much Morton)

1 cup (8 ounces) Philadelphia cream cheese, room-temp so it's nice and soft

Combine the feta and salt in a food processor, then add the cream cheese in several blobs (it's easier on your machine that way). Buzz, occasionally stopping and scraping down the sides if need be, until it's smooth and there are no signs of little pebbly chunks of feta. It'll take 2 to 3 minutes, depending on how soft your cream cheese was.

It keeps in the fridge until the expiration date on the feta or cream cheese.

HOW TO MAKE OVER FROZEN PEAS

I love eating peas. I love eating peas with gravy. Alas, pea season and gravy season aren't the same. So we came up with this hack for frozen peas, which are already pretty good, to make them taste more like awesome shelled, blanched fresh ones. Once they're cured in salt and sugar, they're ready to whirl (see page 71), chile-crunchify (see page 65), or use in salads (see page 57). **MAKES ABOUT 3 CUPS**

Mix **1 tablespoon kosher salt** (Diamond Crystal or about half as much Morton) and **1½ teaspoons white sugar** in a medium mixing bowl, then add **3 cups (16-ounce bag) thawed frozen peas** and stir well. Let them hang out for at least 1 hour or overnight in the fridge. Drain off any liquid that collects in the bowl. Taste, and if they're a little too salty for your taste, give them a brief rinse.

They keep in the fridge for up to 3 days.

OKRANOMIYAKI

I named this dish way before I ever made it. Because I love okonomiyaki—the savory Japanese pancakes topped with Kewpie mayo, sweet-salty sauce, and bonito flakes—and the play on words was too tempting to resist. In my concoction, a bed of roasty, crisp-edged okra gets topped with those same badass Japanese garnishes.

You can buy them online or at a Japanese market. Having these items in your pantry will massively upgrade your snacking, since they make almost anything taste awesome.

SERVES 4

2 pounds okra

¼ cup vegetable oil

1 tablespoon plus 1½ teaspoons kosher salt (Diamond Crystal or about half as much Morton)

¼ cup plus 2 tablespoons okonomi sauce (I like the Otafuku brand)

¼ cup Kewpie mayo

¼ cup plus 2 tablespoons aonori (seaweed flakes)

¼ cup plus 2 tablespoons bonito flakes (katsuobushi)

2 tablespoons toasted sesame seeds

2 scallions, trimmed and thinly sliced (on the diagonal if you're feeling fancy)

¼ cup slivered beni shoga (Japanese red pickled ginger)

Get your oven to 375°F.

Slice the okra lengthwise into about five slices (about ⅛ inch thick each). There's no need to trim off the stems unless they're looking real gnarly.

Toss the okra slices in a large mixing bowl with the oil and salt to coat them well. Scatter them onto two baking sheets in a single layer (some over-lapping slices is no big deal) and roast, rotating the pan halfway through, until they turn beef-jerky brown at the edges but are still soft in the center, 30 to 40 minutes.

Put the okra on a plate—get in there with a thin spatula if your little okra babies decided to stick to the pan—so there's not much empty space. Then evenly zigzag the okonomi sauce and mayo on top. Scatter with the aonori, bonito flakes, sesame seeds, and scallions. Serve with the ginger on the side.

4 Delta Folly

SOME SEAFOOD

CATFISH BLUES

This one is a sort of tuna-salad-on-toast situation, but better because it's made with catfish cooked to happy hell on a grill and topped with lime-y, fish sauce–y grilled kale. I'm of the opinion that you can't have too much horseradish on top, so go large. Serve the bread on the side and you have a dip. Ditch the bread altogether and you have a salad (but maybe don't do that).

Fresh catfish is recommended, as frozen can be a little gnarly. Flounder, trout, and cod work here, too. If you don't have malt vinegar in your pantry, now's the time to get some. It rocks and its nutty flavor is just right for this salad.

To make the catfish salad: Get your grill really hot. Rub the oil on the fillets and season all over with the salt and pepper. Grill 'em, uncovered and flipping once, until they've got dark grill marks and they're well done, 4 to 6 minutes total. Scrape the fish onto a plate (it's OK if it falls apart) and let it cool.

Mix together the sour cream, fish sauce, malt vinegar, lime juice, and jalapeño in a medium mixing bowl, add the cooled catfish, and mix it all up to chunky tuna-salad texture. If you want, add more salt and pepper.

To grill that kale: Toss the kale in a big bowl with the olive oil, salt, and pepper. Grill the kale in more or less a single layer, flipping once, until it's charred in spots, 30 seconds to 1 minute. Let it cool on a plate.

To assemble that dish: Just before you serve, stir together the lime juice, fish sauce, rice vinegar, and sriracha in a small bowl to make a dressing.

Drizzle the oil on both sides of the bread. Grill 'em or toast 'em on a hot griddle in batches until both sides are golden brown, 1 minute or so per side. When they're done, move them to a rack or stand them up so they lean against each other to keep from getting soggy.

Tear the kale into 2-inch-ish pieces, add it to a mixing bowl, and toss with the cilantro, parsley, onion, and dressing. It'll be overdressed. That's real nice here.

Halve the toasts and top them with the catfish salad, then the kale salad, drizzling on any lingering dressing. Use a Microplane to grate the horseradish generously over each one. Eat.

MAKES 12

Catfish Salad

3 tablespoons extra-virgin olive oil

1½ pounds fresh catfish fillets

1 tablespoon kosher salt (Diamond Crystal or about half as much Morton), or more if you like

1 tablespoon freshly ground black pepper, or more if you like

½ cup sour cream

2 tablespoons fish sauce

2 tablespoons malt vinegar

1 tablespoon fresh lime juice

1 jalapeño, finely chopped

Kale

6 ounces stemmed kale

1 tablespoon olive oil

1 teaspoon kosher salt (Diamond Crystal or about half as much Morton)

1 teaspoon freshly ground black pepper

For the Dish

5 tablespoons fresh lime juice

2 tablespoons fish sauce

2 tablespoons unseasoned rice vinegar

1 tablespoon Huy Fong Foods Sriracha

6 tablespoons olive oil

6 thick slices soft white bread

Big ol' handful of roughly chopped cilantro

Small handful of roughly chopped parsley

Some thinly sliced red onion

One 2-inch chunk horseradish, peeled

CRAB CAKE MUFFS

OK, technically this a sandwich, because putting things on bread is almost always a solid idea. But the crab cake is the headliner here. The keys are really nice lump crabmeat, keeping those lumps intact by using a cherub's touch when you mix the ingredients, and giving the mix some time in the fridge, so the saltines have a chance to bind it all together.

White bread's fine, but my buddy Big Bob O'Donnell says that up North they serve crab cakes on English muffins. I tried it and it's definitely the pro move. Whether you choose one, the other, or none at all, do consider serving your crab cakes with zesty buttermilk dressing and a giant squeeze of lemon.

To make the crab cakes: About an hour before you start to cook, whisk together the egg, mayo, Old Bay, tarragon, and salt in a small bowl. In a medium bowl, use your hands to gently toss together the crackers and crab. Fold in the mayo mixture with a delicate touch to keep those lovely crab lumps intact the best you can. Fridge it for at least an hour (so the saltines turn into food glue) or up to a day.

Separate the crab mixture into four blobs, then lightly pack them into 1-inch-or-so-thick patties that are about as wide as the English muffins, and put them on a plate.

Get a large heavy skillet hot over high heat, then add the oil and give it a swirl. When it smokes, add the patties with a little space between each one. Lower the heat to medium and cook until these babies are pancake brown on both sides and hot through, about 4 minutes per side. Move them to a plate. Scrape up any stuck, crispy bits of crab cake and eat them.

To assemble the muffs: Mix the buttermilk dressing and tarragon in a little bowl and let it hang out.

Put the skillet back over medium heat. Generously butter the cut sides of the English muffins, then cook them in batches, cut-side down, until they're nice and toasty, 2 to 3 minutes. Set them aside.

Squeeze the whole lemon all over the crab cakes, then make sandwiches on the English muffins with the crab cakes, tarragon sauce, and shrettuce. Eat with the hot sauce handy, in case anyone's feeling spicy.

Crab Cakes

1 egg

¼ cup mayo
(Duke's or bust)

1 tablespoon
Old Bay Seasoning

1 tablespoon
chopped tarragon

½ teaspoon kosher salt
(Diamond Crystal or about
half as much Morton)

10 saltine crackers,
crushed real small (like
coarse bread crumbs)

1 pound fresh jumbo lump
crabmeat, picked through
for lingering hard stuff

1 tablespoon vegetable oil

Muffs

¼ cup Big Zesty Buttermilk
Dressing (page 226)

2 tablespoons finely
chopped tarragon

2 tablespoons unsalted
butter, room-temp so
it's mayo-soft

4 English muffins, split

1 juicy lemon

1 cup shrettuce
(see page 229)

Louisiana-style hot sauce
for serving

ROE A LA JIFFY

This is an awesome recipe for spoonbread, so easy and so satisfying. It comes straight off a box of muffin mix from Jiffy, the Michigan-based brand that's been selling baking mixes for going on ninety years. My only embellishments for this cake-like cornmeal pudding are just enough tweaks to avoid litigation and the toppings, which contribute salt, fat, acid, and crunch.

SERVES 12

1 cup sour cream

1 stick (8 tablespoons) unsalted butter, melted

1 cup (8¾-ounce can) drained whole kernel corn

1 cup (8¾-ounce can) cream-style corn

2 eggs, lightly beaten

One 8½-ounce package Jiffy Corn Muffin Mix

2 teaspoons kosher salt (Diamond Crystal or about half as much Morton)

1½ cups Anchovy Crème Fraîche (page 224) or sour cream

2 cups potato sticks (like the Utz brand)

4 ounces paddlefish roe, salmon roe, or your favorite fish eggs

⅓ cup very thinly sliced chives

2 lemons, for zesting

Get your oven to 375°F. Grease a 2-quart casserole dish, baking pan, or deep-dish pie plate.

Combine the sour cream, melted butter, corn kernels, cream-style corn, and eggs in the dish and stir well. Add the muffin mix and salt and stir until it's well combined. Bake, rotating the dish halfway through, until a small knife inserted in the center comes out clean, 35 to 40 minutes. Let the spoonbread cool for 20 minutes or so.

When you're ready to serve, scoop out portions of roughly the same size and put them on a platter. Top each with the crème fraîche, potato sticks, roe, and chives. Use a Microplane to zest the lemons evenly over them. Eat.

LOBSTER TOSTADAS

MAKES 8

I got invited to do a guest chef spot at La Docena, a kick-ass New Orleans–style oyster bar in Mexico City, and I spent a solid half of my trip stuffing my face with seafood tostadas. I ate them in nice restaurants, like the fucking perfect Contramar, and in busy markets, where you just grab a stool and watch heaps of octopus, shrimp, and crab land on crispy tortillas.

That trip led to a pop-up series at Turkey and the Wolf where chefs, like Fermín Nuñez and Claudette Zepeda; came and cooked and partied. They cooked cooler food than I did, but I did come up with one dish that I keep coming back to—this lobster tostada with a not-so-Mexican chipotle salsa situation and very-not-Mexican sauce (that I like to think I invented) for which you brown some butter, stir in Old bay, and mix it with mayo. For cooking and picking the lobster meat, I strongly suggest you just Google it, because I cook for a living and that's what I did, and it worked swimmingly. You can also buy it that way or use some nice Gulf shrimp or blue crab.

Old Bay–Brown Butter Mayo

2 tablespoons unsalted butter

1 tablespoon Old Bay Seasoning

½ cup mayo (Duke's or bust)

2 tablespoons fresh lemon juice, or more if you like

Kosher salt

Tostadas

1 pound picked, chopped lobster meat (from about 5 pounds whole lobsters), chilled

Kosher salt

½ cup Chipotle Romesco (page 88), at room temp, or some chipotle hot sauce

8 store-bought tostadas

1 large celery stalk, very thinly sliced

Some thinly sliced red onion

Handful of basil leaves, preferably Thai, torn at the last minute

1 cup loosely packed roughly chopped cilantro

2 juicy lemons, cut into wedges

To make the mayo: Melt the butter in a small heavy skillet over medium heat, using a wooden spoon to keep it moving. Once the butter is melted, swirl almost constantly until it turns somewhere between honey and caramel brown (to see the color in a dark skillet, you might need to tip the skillet and/or push away the froth), about 3 minutes. Turn off the heat and keep swirling until the butter turns a shade darker and smells nutty.

Add the Old Bay to the butter, stir well, then let the mixture cool in the skillet. Dump it into a bowl, stir in the mayo and lemon juice, then season with salt and more lemon juice until you're happy. It keeps in the fridge for up to 2 weeks.

To assemble the tostadas: Mix the lobster meat and a heaping ¼ cup of the mayo in a bowl (save the rest for a bag of Ruffles), stir to coat, and season with salt until you're happy.

Evenly spread 1 tablespoon of the romesco over each tostada (if you're using hot sauce, dash it all over), then divide the lobster among them. Sprinkle on the celery and onion, then the basil and cilantro. Serve with the lemon wedges for squeezing.

Eat it.

CHIPOTLE ROMESCO

I'm well known among my kitchen colleagues for diving into some "eureka" sauce idea—to their dismay, often in the middle of service—then when the sauce doesn't quite work, getting lost in trying to fix it. When I'm lucky, I fall face-first into a keeper. That's what happened here, when my attempt at a smoky salsa ended up as this Frankenstein romesco.

Lobster tostadas love it. So do raw vegetables looking for a dip. My wife loves it on baked sweet potatoes with some butter, feta, chopped almonds, and basil. **Makes about 1½ cups**

Combine all the ingredients in your blender, add ¼ cup plus 1 tablespoon water, and blend until it's as smooth as you can make it. If you have a shitty blender, you might need to gradually add a little extra water to get everything mixing. Season with more salt until you're happy.

It keeps in an airtight container in the fridge for up to 1 month.

¾ cup salted roasted almonds

½ cup extra-virgin olive oil

¼ cup distilled white vinegar

2 teaspoons dried minced garlic

1 teaspoon kosher salt (Diamond Crystal or about half as much Morton), or more if you like

1 teaspoon dried oregano

4 canned chipotles in adobo, plus a scant 1 tablespoon of the adobo sauce

HOT TUNA

This stuff is basically just dope tuna salad loaded with some pickle-y crunch. One time, I ate an entire quart of it. It's spicy hot, not temperature hot, but the confusion is worth it to salute the excellent band Hot Tuna. Serve it with a soundtrack of Genesis and some crusty bread or Ritz crackers, or just wash your hands and eat it off your fingers.

SERVES 10 (AS A PARTY SNACK)

Put the giardiniera in a small mixing bowl. Use a Microplane to zest one of the lemons over the giardiniera, then halve the lemons and squeeze in the juice of one of the halves. Stir well and set aside.

Dump the tuna (oil and all) into a medium mixing bowl and break up into little chunks with a fork. Use a Microplane to grate the garlic and jalapeño into the bowl. It's fine if some chile seeds get in there. Add the mayo, black pepper, salt, and fish sauce, then squeeze in a couple of tablespoons lemon juice. Stir and mash really well until it's as smooth as deli tuna salad. Season with more salt and lemon juice until you're happy.

Put the tuna salad in a serving bowl or on a plate and spoon in the giardiniera mixture. Top with the Calabrian chiles, then the dill and basil. Serve it alongside bread or crackers.

Scant ½ cup drained jarred Chicago-style hot giardiniera

2 juicy lemons, for zesting and juicing

Two 5-ounce cans oil-packed tuna

2 garlic cloves, peeled

1 jalapeño

½ cup mayo (Duke's or bust)

2 teaspoons freshly ground black pepper, or more if you like

1 teaspoon kosher salt (Diamond Crystal or about half as much Morton), or more if you like

1 teaspoon fish sauce

1 teaspoon crushed Calabrian chiles, or ½ teaspoon red chile flakes

¼ cup lightly packed picked dill

10 or so basil leaves, torn

Crusty bread or Ritz crackers for serving

HOW WE EAT SARDINES

A party platter fueled by deluxe bagel flavors but with canned sardines as the showcase. Buy the expensive ones if you're feeling plush, but I'm pretty sure all canned sardines are delicious.

If you're not a sardine person, you've got some things to work out, but feel free to sub smoked salmon or a can of tuna. Alternatively, ditch the fish altogether and eat the magical trimmings with roasted veg or get weird and mix all the stuff into the cream cheese and smear it on toast.

Arrange the ingredients on a platter, squeeze lemon juice over everything but the chips, and go at it.

A few cans of oil-packed sardines

Some Chimichurri Cream Cheese (recipe follows)

Some thinly sliced white onion

Some picked parsley leaves

Some chopped hot pickled cherry peppers

Some drained capers

Some dill pickle spears

A large bag of your favorite bagel, pita, or potato chips

1 juicy lemon

CHIMICHURRI CREAM CHEESE

Sure, the combo of cream cheese and chimichurri-adjacent herb sauce sounds good, but when you make it, you realize it's even better than you expected. This stuff is surprisingly versatile—meant for a sardine snack attack (above)—but awesome on anything from a plain bagel to cooked fish. Bonus: Mixing your herby sauce into cream cheese keeps it kicking way longer. **Makes about 1½ cups**

Put the cream cheese in a food processor in several blobs (it's easier on your machine that way), then add the blender sauce and salt. Buzz until smooth. Season with more salt until you're happy.

It keeps in the fridge for up to 1 week, or until the expiration date on the cream cheese.

2 cups (1 pound) Philadelphia cream cheese, room-temp so it's nice and soft

1 cup Verdant Blender Sauce (page 216)

1 teaspoon kosher salt (Diamond Crystal or about half as much Morton), or more if you like

MCCAVIAR

I'm always seeing caviar and crème fraîche on top of crispy potatoes at high-end restaurants. I want in on the action, because if you ask me, this crunchy, creamy, salty snack is what dreams are made of. Deep-frying hash brown patties is tried and true; but here, I'd sooner swing by a fast-food joint and buy some hash browns. And honestly, Sour Cream & Onion Pringles are awesome stand-ins for the hash browns.

MAKES 8

Vegetable oil for deep-frying (about 2 quarts; optional but optimal)

8 frozen hash brown patties (if you didn't buy them hot)

Kosher salt

½ to 1 cup Anchovy Crème Fraîche (page 224)

2 ounces paddlefish roe, salmon roe, or your favorite fish eggs

¼ cup very thinly sliced chives

½ juicy lemon

If you didn't buy hot hash browns: Bring 2 inches of oil to 350°F. In batches, add the frozen hash browns and fry, flipping once, until they're deep golden brown, 4 to 5 minutes per batch. While you're frying, get your oven to 250°F and line a baking sheet with a wire rack or paper towels. Move the hash browns to the baking sheet, immediately season both sides with salt, and put in the oven to keep warm while you fry the rest.

If you did buy hot hash browns: Stick the hot hash browns in a 400°F oven to warm them up.

Once the hash browns are all done, move them to a platter. Spoon a tablespoon or two of the anchovy crème fraîche on each hash brown, distribute the fish eggs, sprinkle with the chives, and squeeze on a little lemon juice. Eat.

SHRIMP WITH GRAPES AND NUTS

One time in Miami, I enjoyed a ceviche with mayo in it. When I realized that was a thing, there was no going back; because as you might have noticed, adding mayo to stuff is a bit of a theme in this book. Some grapes and macadamia nuts make it, as my lady tells me, "weird but in a really good way"—my favorite kind of compliment. It requires top-notch shrimp (or slivered white-fleshed fish, like snapper, sea bass, or yellowtail, or sliced scallops), so this is no time for Walmart, my friends. I serve mine with tortilla chips, tostadas, or some spoons, and a bottle of habanero hot sauce.

To prep the shrimp: Put the shrimp in a single layer on a plate or two and season evenly with the salt (just on one side is fine). Refrigerate for at least 15 minutes or up to 2 hours.

To blend the sauce: Combine the lime juice, onion, cilantro, verjus, mayo, fish sauce, salt, serrano, pequin chile, and chopped cucumber in a blender and blend on high speed until smooth, about 20 seconds. It's ready to go, or you can keep it in the fridge for up to 2 hours.

To serve: Combine the shrimp and sauce in a serving bowl. Add the nuts, grapes, cilantro, sliced cucumber, and red onion and stir well. Taste for salt and add a bit more, if you want. I probably would.

FEEDS 6 TO 8 (AS A PARTY SNACK)

Shrimp

1 pound super-fresh peeled, deveined shrimp, halved lengthwise

1 tablespoon kosher salt (Diamond Crystal or about half as much Morton)

Sauce

½ cup fresh lime juice (from 4 to 6 limes)

Heaping 2 tablespoons chopped white onion

Scant ¼ cup roughly chopped cilantro

2 tablespoons verjus, or 1 tablespoon unseasoned rice vinegar mixed with 1 teaspoon honey

2 tablespoons mayo (Duke's or bust)

1½ teaspoons fish sauce

1 teaspoon kosher salt (Diamond Crystal or about half as much Morton)

1 serrano or jalapeño, stemmed

½ dried pequin chile, or pinch of red chile flakes

½ medium cucumber, roughly chopped

For Serving

½ cup salted roasted macadamia nuts or almonds, roughly chopped

½ cup thinly sliced or quartered grapes

½ cup packed roughly chopped cilantro

1 medium cucumber, halved and thinly sliced

¼ cup sliced red onion

Kosher salt

For The Best Seafood In Town

SUE'S SEAFOOD

(504)348-9394   Stall #5

FRESH CRAB MEAT • OYSTERS • FILLET FISH • GUMBO CRABS • SOFT SHELL • TURTLE MEAT • ALLIGATOR MEAT • PEELED SHRIMP • FROG LEGS

SUE'S
SEAFOOD

SHRIMP

FRESH
OYSTERS | FRESH
CRAB
MEAT

BAGS/CASES
OF
FILLET
FISH

ENJOY Every SANDW

A WORD ABOUT BREAD

When David Letterman asked dying rock legend Warren Zevon if there was anything he understood now that he was faced with his own mortality, Zevon replied, "Just how much you're supposed to enjoy every sandwich."

For some reason, when you put a slice of bread on either side of a good meal, people take it less seriously. This is mostly good, because we should take a lot of things less seriously. Yet the greatness of the sandwich shouldn't be underestimated.

One thing I love about serving sandwiches is that they offer an opportunity to craft every bite of someone's meal. Think about it. Serve some chicken, a couple of sides, and some sauce on a plate and people will choose their own adventure, eating a bite of this with a little of that. But with a great sandwich, you take the same elements that make a great plate of food—the acid and fat, the temperatures and textures, the salt and sauciness—and spread, arrange, and layer them between bread so that each bite is preordained. A sandwich is the sum total of a meal's greatness served as the best bite over and over again.

In other words, sandwiches deserve the same care as any composed dish. The bread included.

CHOOSE YOUR BREAD WISELY.

Bread isn't just a vehicle, it's a component. Consider its crustiness and toastability, its density and size and flavor. Don't use wheat bread just because it seems healthier. Use it because you've thought strategically about how its subtle sweetness will bond with its cheese-sauce-topping family. Don't use rye just because you bought a loaf; let that rye direct your sandwich-making adventures.

Thickness is another important quality to consider. When this book calls for white bread, we're talking sweet, squishy, square sandwich bread. Problem is, it's tough to find presliced white bread that's sliced thick enough to achieve what I love from a butter-toast—the crackly, crisp exterior and the soft, steamy, chewy interior. To get those two distinct textures, I say try to buy whole loaves from a local bakery—buying stuff from your neighbors is cool, too, and the pain de mie or pullman loaf you get will probably taste and toast great—and slice it yourself to about 1½ inches thick. If that fails, a little searching at the grocery store will turn up loaves (Bunny TexToast and Martin's Butter Bread, to name two) that are presliced to ¾ to 1 inch thick. And that's pretty good.

TOAST IT IN A PAN, REST IT LIKE A STEAK.

Whether you use butter, olive oil, or some other cool fat, toasting bread in a pan gives it a crisp exterior and a tender, chewy interior. It gives you the best-looking, best-smelling, best-tasting crust. It also rejuvenates day-three bread better than any other method, if you ask me.

After bread toasts, it must rest. I was taught this by the wise Colleen Quarls, our opening chef de cuisine at Turkey and the Wolf. She discovered that going straight into the sandwich build after toasting creates suboptimum architecture—the bottom slice gets trapped between the toppings and the cutting board, sogging out and compromising the structural integrity.

The answer is to rest the toasted bread on a wire rack or, if you don't have one, lean your two pieces of toast against each other like an "A." That way, the bread has a chance to breathe so it can retain its crisp exterior and become tectonically sound sandwich toast.

THE BELLAIR (THE REASON WE MAKE SANDWICHES)

I built this, the ham sandwich of my dreams, with one thing on my mind: The Jefferson at Bellair Market, in Charlottesville, Virginia, where I grew up. It's been my favorite sandwich ever since I was old enough to make lofty statements like "this is my favorite sandwich ever." The main difference, really, is that we use our house-made city ham (not country ham) instead of turkey. Otherwise, it's the same components—the herby mayo, the schmear of cranberry, the sharp cheddar. We even buy the French roll from the same bakery they do.

And yeah, I masochistically read Internet comment sections, so I know I'm a punk-ass poser for ripping off someone else's sandwich. Still, I love this thing. And Bellair has since added a sandwich to their menu based on the Turkey and the Wolf bologna sandwich. They named it "A Touch of Mason." Highlight of my life right there.

MAKES 4

Four 8-inch French or hoagie rolls, split

½ cup Ocean Spray Jellied Cranberry Sauce

Heaping ½ cup Bellair-Style Herb Mayo (page 218)

1 pound sliced (ideally ⅛ inch thick) smoky ham

4 cups nice spicy arugula

8 ounces super-sharp cheddar, sliced ⅛ inch thick

Move an oven rack 8 inches or so from your broiler and preheat the broiler. Toast the rolls, cut-sides up, under the broiler for a minute or so, just until they're golden brown and crackly but still soft inside.

Give the cranberry sauce a good stir so it's spreadable, then spread it on the top halves of each roll. Spread the herb mayo on the bottom halves.

For each sandwich, put a fourth of the ham on the roll bottoms (feel free to artistically fold each slice like they do at Subway). Pile on about 1 cup of the arugula (it's a lot, so just try your best to tuck it in there). Then puzzle-piece on a fourth of the cheese in an even layer with minimal overhang. Throw the tops on those bad boys and eat.

THE COLLARD MELT

I'm a bit biased, but the best sandwich shop in New Orleans is Stein's Market & Deli, a few blocks away from Turkey and the Wolf. (You'll meet the owner, sandwich king, and my dear friend Dan in hot dog form on page 186.) When we set out to make a sandwich with collards, we had The Sam (Stein's hot pastrami with Swiss, coleslaw, and Russian dressing on rye) dancing in our heads.

We swapped in stewed collards for pastrami, added a little heat to the dressing, and made it a triple decker—an accidental but vital modification for our version. We intended to use two thick slices of rye, but our bread purveyor sent us regular slices, so we added a third for balance. When one of our regulars tried it, he went on and on about the middle "soaker slice," which really does kinda slurp up all the dressing and slaw juice to make a mega-tasty safeguard of structural soundness. Now it's a three-slicer forever.

To make the slaw: Combine the coleslaw ingredients in a large mixing bowl and mix really well with your hands, massaging the cabbage so it wilts to about 3 cups of coleslaw. I like it cold, so consider chilling it in the fridge, where it keeps for up to 3 days. Before you use it, taste and add more vinegar and salt, if you want.

To assemble the sandwiches: Move an oven rack so it's 4 to 6 inches from your broiler and preheat the broiler. Heat up the collards, along with a splash of pot likker or water to keep things juicy, in a small pot.

Get a well-seasoned cast-iron skillet or griddle good and hot over medium heat. Swipe the butter on each side of the bread and toast in batches in the skillet until both sides are golden brown, 1 to 2 minutes per side.

Once they're all toasted, move twelve of the slices of rye to a baking sheet or two in a single layer, top each with a slice of cheese, and melt the cheese under the broiler, 1 to 2 minutes.

Put a handful of the coleslaw on six of the cheesy slices of rye, top with the other cheesy slices (cheese-side up), then spoon on the collard greens (about ¼ cup per sandwich, or more if you like). Slather the remaining slices of rye with the Russian dressing and complete the sandwiches. By now, they'll be room temp, which is how the Turkey and the Wolf crew likes them. Halve them and eat them.

MAKES 6

Coleslaw

6 cups packed thinly sliced green cabbage

Heaping ½ cup mayo (Duke's or bust)

¼ cup thinly sliced white onion

1½ tablespoons distilled white vinegar, or more if you like

1 teaspoon kosher salt (Diamond Crystal or about half as much Morton), or more if you like

¾ teaspoon freshly ground black pepper

Sandwiches

1½ cups Scotty's Good-with-Everything Collard Greens (page 178), or more if you like

2 sticks (16 tablespoons) unsalted butter, room-temp so it's mayo-soft

18 slices seeded soft rye bread

12 thick-cut (⅛ inch) slices Swiss cheese

Spicy Russian Dressing (page 225) for slathering

THE 86'D CHICKEN-FRIED STEAK

The first national press that Turkey and the Wolf ever received was an article by a big-time restaurant critic named Bill Addison. He said some really nice things that to this day make me blush. Including that this sandwich arguably ranks as our greatest creation. I can't believe anyone has ranked *any* of our creations.

The day the article came out, we 86'd the "undisputed star of the menu." Partly so it could go out on a high note, George Costanza–style, and partly to fight the expectations game. Better to undersell and overdeliver, if you ask me. But that sandwich makes its return right here, exactly how we made it at the restaurant: pickles, slaw, pepper jelly, and crispy, crackly chicken-fried steak. On bread or on a plate, the steak is extra nice because we pound the hell out of it (more surface area = more tasty dredge), we dredge it twice, and as soon as it leaves the hot oil, we hit it with chicken salt, a two-ingredient secret to unlocking new levels in the video game that is your tongue.

To prep the steak: One by one, put the steak slices between pieces of plastic wrap, put them on a cutting board, and use a meat mallet, rolling pin, or bottom of a small sturdy skillet to evenly pound the hell out of them, so they're very thin (like, ⅛ inch at most). It's totally OK if they get holes or tear a bit.

Grab two medium mixing bowls. Pour the buttermilk into one. In the other, stir together the flour, garlic powder, paprika, black pepper, kosher salt, onion powder, and chicken bouillon.

One by one, toss the steak slices in the flour mixture, patting to make sure each is evenly coated. Next, shake off any excess coating and submerge in the buttermilk. Let any excess drip back into the bowl and toss the steak in the flour mixture again, patting to evenly coat. As they're done, put the slices on a plate. They're ready to fry now, but they can hang out, uncovered, in the fridge for up to 12 hours.

continued

SLICING THAT STEAK

Ask nice and a butcher will probably slice your steak for you. If you're shy or you forget to ask, it's easy to do yourself. A very sharp knife helps and so does briefly freezing the steak so it's nice and firm and therefore easier to cut into thin, even slices.

MAKES 4

Chicken-Fried Steak

1 pound boneless strip or sirloin steak, fat cap trimmed, cut horizontally into 4 slices (see "Slicing that Steak")

1 cup buttermilk

3 cups all-purpose flour

2½ tablespoons garlic powder

1 tablespoon plus 1 teaspoon smoked paprika

1 tablespoon freshly ground black pepper

2¼ teaspoons kosher salt (Diamond Crystal or about half as much Morton)

1 teaspoon onion powder

1 teaspoon granulated chicken bouillon (preferably Totole brand, see "Chicken Powder"; optional but optimal)

Sandwiches

Vegetable oil for deep-frying (about 2 quarts)

1 tablespoon Chicken Salt (page 231), or more if you like

6 tablespoons unsalted butter, room-temp so it's mayo-soft

8 thick slices soft white bread

Bird Sauce (page 112) for swiping

Your favorite pepper jelly for swiping

2 cups coleslaw (see page 106)

20 or so drained dill pickle chips

ENJOY EVERY SANDWICH

To assemble the sandwiches:
Get 2 inches of oil to 350°F in a large heavy pot over medium-high heat. Line a baking sheet with a wire rack or paper towels.

Working in two batches, fry the steaks, flipping them once, until they're golden brown and super-crispy, like fried chicken, 5 to 6 minutes per batch. When they're done, use tongs to move them to the baking sheet and season immediately on both sides with the chicken salt. (Sneak a bite and add more chicken salt, if you want.)

Get a well-seasoned cast-iron skillet or griddle good and hot over medium heat. Swipe the butter on each side of the bread and toast in batches in the skillet until both sides are golden brown, 1 to 2 minutes per side. When they're done, move them to a rack or stand them up so they lean against each other to keep from getting soggy.

Generously swipe bird sauce on four of the toasted bread slices and swipe a generous amount of pepper jelly on the other four. Top each pepper jelly–slathered slice with ½ cup coleslaw, then the steak, then some pickle chips. Add the bird sauce–slathered slices and get wild.

CHICKEN POWDER

There are many options out there, but I love Totole brand granulated chicken flavor soup base mix with my whole heart. It's science-created, like pure MSG, except it has chicken flavor, so it's even better. When I travel to cook, it travels with me. Buy it online or look for it at Asian markets. If you're afraid of bouillon powder, MSG, or flavor, you can totally leave it out, though you'll probably want to add a little extra salt.

BIRD SAUCE

Between the crunchy dredge and the fresh-out-the-oil shower of chicken salt, our chicken-fried steak sandwich had folks convinced it was straight-up poultry. And they have a point. When we were conceiving this one, all that fried-bird flavor got me thinking of dunking drums and thighs from McHardy's Chicken & Fixin', a takeout spot in the Seventh Ward that makes my favorite fried chicken in the city, in their zingy Cluck Sauce, which it turns out I've been incorrectly referring to for years as "bird sauce," and which inspired this easy, awesome bread spread. **Makes about 1 cup**

1 cup mayo (Duke's or bust)

Several dashes Louisiana-style hot sauce

Several dashes Worcestershire sauce

½ teaspoons kosher salt (Diamond Crystal or about half as much Morton)

Generous 2 pinches freshly ground black pepper

A squeeze of lemon juice, or more if you like

Mix up all the ingredients in a bowl. Season with more lemon juice until you're happy.

It'll keep the fridge for up to 1 week.

DUKE'S OR BUST

I have a Duke's mayonnaise tattoo. I was in a Duke's commercial. In retrospect, "churched-up Duke's" should've been an entire chapter in my original business plan. It is the undisputed king of mayo, tangier and more velvety than the others. So you know what I think you should be spreading—edge to edge, corner to corner—on your sandwiches. When slathering, listen to your heart, keeping in mind that adding more than is socially acceptable is almost always correct.

CUTTING BOARD SALAD

Towers of chips, pickle slices teetering atop heaps of shredded iceberg, the 1990s worth of arugula—we like to overload our sandwiches and tostadas and just about everything else we make. So much so, that perching that piece of bread on top or taking that first precarious bite triggers an avalanche onto your cutting board. Do not despair. Now you have cutting board salad. The rubble—a shard of crunchy tortilla slicked with mayo, a tangle of cheesy sauerkraut dripping with Russian dressing, an escaped pickle capped with slaw—serves as a lovely appetizer before you dig in properly or as a consolation to ease the disappointment of having taken the last bite of a delicious sandwich.

ENJOY EVERY SANDWICH

THE TOMATO

This might catch me shade from some Southerners, but my favorite tomato sandwich ain't the classic made with just tomatoes, mayo, salt, and pepper. It's this one.

Don't worry, though, I'm not on some chef shit where I tell you to batter and fry something or make aioli. But you should go extra hard on ingredients that make good tomatoes taste extra awesome. So slather way too much mayo on butter-toasted bread, pile on a comical amount of herbs, squeeze on a goddamn downpour of lemon juice, and add more buttery little sunflower seeds than anyone has ever seen on a sandwich, which I guess isn't saying much since you don't really see sunflower seeds on sandwiches that aren't this one.

Get a well-seasoned cast-iron skillet or griddle good and hot over medium heat. Swipe the butter on each side of the bread and toast in batches in the skillet until both sides are golden brown, 1 to 2 minutes per side. When they're done, move them to a rack or stand them up so they lean against each other to keep from getting soggy.

Spread the mayo evenly on one side of each slice of bread, consider adding more because tomatoes love mayo, then sprinkle the sunflower seeds on four of the slices. Sprinkle the salt and lots of pepper on both sides of the tomato slices, then pile them on the bread slices that have sunflower seeds. Top the tomatoes with the herbs (it's a lot, so just try your best to tuck them in there and don't sweat it if they fall onto the plate). Squeeze on every last drop of juice from the lemons.

Top with the rest of the bread. Cut it in half if you want. Instagram it, and tag your mom. Eat.

MAKES 4

6 tablespoons unsalted butter, room-temp so it's mayo-soft

8 thick slices white bread, preferably 1 inch thick

½ cup mayo (Duke's or bust), or more if you like

1 cup roasted salted hulled sunflower seeds

1 tablespoon kosher salt (Diamond Crystal or about half as much Morton)

Freshly ground black pepper

2 pounds juicy, ripe tomatoes, cored and cut across into ½-inch slices

Big ol' handful of basil leaves

Handful of picked dill

2 juicy lemons, halved

THE ITALIAN-AMERICAN

The city of New Orleans already had the muffaletta perfected, so we took on a different Italian-American sandwich, the kind piled with thinly sliced cured pork products, shrettuce, and pickled peppers, then dressed with olive and vinegar. I had eaten my share of such subs in Charlottesville, but it was former Philly cat Scotty who served as our hoagie authority. He guided our hand—the right medley of deli meat, the right roll (not too crusty, not too soft).

He even green-lit our foray into cream cheese, which turned out to be a great vehicle for all the crucial but peripheral flavors (e.g., spicy peppers, olives in homage to the muffaletta, and feta for a G-rated stand-in for the classic aged provolone bite). It earned a two-year tenure at Turkey and the Wolf and resurrection at Molly's on a bagel, which FYI totally makes it okay to eat for breakfast. Add a couple of olives speared on toothpicks if you don't mind your food looking back at you.

MAKES 6

Six 8-inch hoagie rolls, not split

½ cup mayo (Duke's or bust), or more if you like

1½ pounds thinly sliced mortadella

12 ounces thinly sliced deli soppressata

6 cups shrettuce (see page 229)

2 cups drained sliced hot pickled banana peppers

Some thinly sliced red onion

¾ cup Italian-Sandwich Vinaigrette (page 120), or more if you like

1½ cups Italian-Sandwich Cream Cheese (page 120), room-temp so it's nice and soft

Get your oven to 400°F.

Toast your hoagie rolls for 3 to 5 minutes, so they're a little crackly on the outside and just warm through. Let the rolls cool slightly, then split them lengthwise.

Spread the mayo evenly and thoroughly on the bottom half of each roll, then consider adding more. Evenly layer the mortadella and soppressata on top of the mayo. Add the shrettuce, banana peppers, and onion slices, then spoon on the vinaigrette, about 2 tablespoons per sandwich or more if you're feeling greasy.

Spread the Italian-sandwich cream cheese on the top half of the rolls (about ¼ cup per), top the sandwiches, cut them in half, and eat.

ENJOY EVERY SANDWICH

ITALIAN-SANDWICH VINAIGRETTE

Here's a simple stand-in for a deli Italian vin that's designed for slow-soaking into the bread of the Italian-American (page 119). **Makes 1¼ cups**

Combine everything in a jar or another container with a lid, cover tightly, and shake it up. Add more sherry vinegar and salt until you're happy.

It keeps in the fridge for up to 1 month. Shake again right before you serve it.

1 cup extra-virgin olive oil

3½ tablespoons sherry vinegar, or more if you like

2 tablespoons Louisiana-style hot sauce

1 tablespoon plus 1 teaspoon Italian seasoning

½ teaspoon kosher salt (Diamond Crystal or about half as much Morton), or more if you like

ITALIAN-SANDWICH CREAM CHEESE

Never underestimate cream cheese as a vehicle for flavors you want to add to a sandwich—like the spicy, pickley stuff that makes an Italian sandwich such a joy. We once made a Chicago-style hot dog with all the toppings just chopped up and mixed into cream cheese and even that worked. Fuckin' cream cheese. It's great. **Makes 1½ cups**

Pulse the olive mixture, cherry peppers, and capers in a food processor until they're all finely chopped but not pulverized. Dump them in a mesh strainer, use a spoon to gently press the solids to drain off some of the liquid, then dump the solids in a mixing bowl.

Put the cream cheese in the food processor in several blobs (it's easier on your machine that way), then add the feta and salt and buzz until smooth, about 1 minute. Scrape the cream cheese mixture into the olive-cherry pepper mixture and combine really well. Season with more salt until you're happy.

It keeps in the fridge for up to 1 week or until the expiration date on the cream cheese.

Heaping ½ cup drained pitted spicy olive mixture

½ cup drained sliced hot pickled cherry peppers

⅓ cup drained capers (from a 2-ounce jar)

8 ounces (1 cup) Philadelphia cream cheese, room-temp so it's nice and soft

⅓ cup crumbled feta

½ teaspoon kosher salt (Diamond Crystal or about half as much Morton)

THE SOFTSHELL CRAB

Softshell crabs are the best. They're essentially crabs caught in the nude, after they shed their hard shell and before they form a new one. Found off the Gulf and mid-Atlantic coasts, they're typically available fresh from early spring to fall, but the season is unpredictable, so if you spot them, buy them. To get them on this sandwich, they need a dredge and a swim in hot oil. To make them sing, we slather with Colleen's malt vinegar tartar sauce, pile on shrettuce, and finish with a lemon deluge. Old Bay sprinkled over the top of the bread seals the deal.

MAKES 4

Vegetable oil or canola oil for deep-frying (about 2 quarts)

1 cup all-purpose flour

½ teaspoon kosher salt (Diamond Crystal or about half as much Morton), plus more for sprinkling

½ teaspoon freshly ground black pepper

4 big softshell crabs (5 to 6 ounces each), or 8 smaller ones, prepped (see "Buying and Cleaning Softies," page 124)

6 tablespoons unsalted butter, room-temp so it's mayo-soft

8 thick slices soft white bread

Malt Vinegar Tartar Sauce (page 124) for swiping

2 cups shrettuce (see page 229)

Some thinly sliced white or yellow onion

1 to 2 jalapeños, thinly sliced

1 juicy lemon

Old Bay Seasoning, straight out of the container, for sprinkling

Get 2 inches of oil to 350°F in a large heavy pot over medium-high heat. Line a baking sheet with a wire rack or paper towels.

Stir together the flour, salt, and black pepper in a medium mixing bowl. One at a time, put the crabs in the flour mixture and get in there with your hands to make sure they're totally coated, including underneath the pointy flaps on the top side (where the gills used to be). Give them a light shake, then move them to a plate.

When the oil's ready, fry the crabs in batches, if necessary, so they don't crowd the oil, flipping once halfway through and adjusting the heat to keep the oil temp around 350°F, until they're crispy and the claws and legs are fried in place, 5 to 7 minutes. When they're done, use tongs to move them to the baking sheet and immediately and liberally sprinkle both sides with salt.

Get a large well-seasoned cast-iron or nonstick skillet or griddle good and hot over medium heat. Swipe the butter generously on each side of the bread slices. Working in batches, cook the bread until both sides are golden brown, 1 to 2 minutes per side. When they're done, move them to a rack or stand them up so they lean against each other to keep from getting soggy.

Generously swipe the tartar sauce on all eight slices of bread. Pile the shrettuce on four slices, perch the onions and jalapeños on top, and add your crabs. Squeeze that lemon juice all over the crabs, top with the rest of the bread, and sprinkle with Old Bay to give the tops a thin, even layer of fairy dust. Cut in half and eat.

MALT VINEGAR TARTAR SAUCE

First, my buddy Stew home-brewed a bunch of beer he didn't love, so Colleen fermented it into malt vinegar. Then she turned that vinegar into this banging tartar sauce for the first softshell crabs of the season. Unsurprisingly, this stuff also rules on fried catfish, fish sticks, and fries. It's a good reminder that nutty, caramelly malt vinegar deserves a place in our pantries next to the cider and balsamic. **Makes about 1½ cups**

¼ cup chopped-up-small dill pickle

1 cup mayo (Duke's or bust)

¼ cup malt vinegar

3 tablespoons chopped-up dill

1 teaspoon freshly ground black pepper

½ teaspoon kosher salt (Diamond Crystal or about half as much Morton)

Give the chopped pickle a quick pat with a paper towel. Put it in a bowl with the rest of the ingredients and mix it all up.

It'll keep the fridge for up to 10 days.

BUYING AND CLEANING SOFTIES

Like you would with oysters and clams, you want to buy softshell crabs that are still alive. They take just a bit of prep to get ready for frying. You can ask the seller if they're willing to clean the crabs for you, or do it yourself.

The world wide web is filled with tutorials, but basically you use kitchen scissors to snip off the face area (this kills them, plus you don't want to eat a crab face) and the apron, a.k.a. the little triangular flap on the underside. Next, find the pointy parts on either side of where the face once was, then lift them up and snip off the feathery gills.

The pro move I don't often see online is to use the scissors or a sharp knife to poke around a little through the opening where the face once was to puncture any pockets of air or liquid. If you skip this step, softies might pop-pop-pop while frying, though even if you don't, I recommend a splatter screen and caution so you stay out of the splash zone.

SOFT-ASS BUTTER

Not to be abbreviated as "soft ass" or "ass butter." For many of the sandwiches in this book, you're going to generously spread butter on both sides of bread and then toast them to a golden brown, like my ass after a beach nap in the Aruba sun. So to make the sandwiches in this book, and for a good life in general, always have a stick or two of butter at room temperature so it's as soft as mayo and doesn't tear your tender white bread when you spread it. If you live in Antarctica or it's below 50°F and you're in a city like New Orleans that doesn't fuck with home insulation, you might want to microwave the butter, then brush it on, or just melt plenty of it in a pan and toast the bread in that.

THE BOLOGNA

The bologna sandwich at Turkey and the Wolf took a lot of people to become awesome. We rely on tubed pork from my friends Leighann and Dan's butcher shop Piece of Meat, David Weiss's white bread (which he created for us), and homemade chips that, thanks to a quick pickling, clock in somewhere between salt-and-vinegar and plain. But at the end of the day, it's just a bologna sandwich, and at home you're not going to break your back to make it. Instead you should hit the store and follow your heart. Buy the good bologna (mortadella works, too), select a nice squishy white bread, and grab a bag of chips.

But, and this is important, *do* make the sweet-hot mustard! I inherited the recipe from Tay, my great buddy Via's mom. And when Tay offers you a recipe, you make it, or in my case, you pair it with Duke's mayonnaise and build a restaurant around it.

MAKES 4

6 tablespoons unsalted butter, room-temp so it's mayo-soft

8 thick slices soft white bread

12 thick (about ⅛ inch) slices bologna

8 slices American cheese

Mayo (Duke's or bust) for swiping

Tay's Mustard (page 217) or your favorite sweet-hot mustard for swiping

2 cups shrettuce (see page 229)

4 big ol' handfuls of salt-and-vinegar potato chips

Get your oven to 400°F.

Get a well-seasoned cast-iron skillet or griddle good and hot over medium heat. Swipe the butter on each side of the bread and toast in batches in the skillet until both sides are golden brown, 1 to 2 minutes per side. When they're done, move them to a rack or stand them up so they lean against each other, to keep from getting soggy.

In that same skillet, cook the bologna slices over medium-high heat, in batches if necessary, until nice and brown on both sides, about 2 minutes per side. As they're done, move them to a baking sheet in slightly over-lapping groups of three. When they're all browned, top each group with two slices of the cheese and stick the pan in the oven until the cheese gets melty, about 3 minutes.

Meanwhile, swipe a socially unacceptable amount of mayo on four of the bread slices and swipe a similarly generous amount of mustard on the other four. Add the shrettuce to the mayo-slathered slices, then the cheesy bologna, then a handful of chips so big that half of them fall off.

Cover with the remaining bread slices and press down on each one with your palm, crushing the chips, so the sandwich can just barely fit in a human mouth. Eat.

MEATLOAF: THE SANDWICH, NOT THE MUSICIAN

We didn't totally realize it at the time, but we created this sandwich to fulfill our craving for a Big Mac. Except the beef comes in the form of meatloaf, the special sauce is an in-the-mouth melding of gravy mayo and pepper jelly, and there are sesame seeds but no bun. Just thick, butter-toasted white bread.

MAKES 4

6 tablespoons unsalted butter, room-temp so it's mayo-soft

8 thick slices soft white bread

Eight ½-inch-thick slices meatloaf (see page 33)

8 slices American cheese

⅓ cup Tastes-Like-There's-Gravy-in-It Mayo (recipe follows) or plain mayo

Heaping ¼ cup your favorite pepper jelly

Some thinly sliced white or yellow onion

2 cups shrettuce (see page 229)

24 drained dill pickle chips

Heaping ½ cup toasted sesame seeds

Get your oven to 400°F.

Get a well-seasoned cast-iron skillet or griddle good and hot over medium heat. Swipe the butter on each side of the bread and toast in batches in the skillet until both sides are golden brown, 1 to 2 minutes per side. When they're done, move them to a rack or stand them up so they lean against each other, to keep from getting soggy.

Grab a baking sheet and arrange the meatloaf slices side by side in overlapping pairs so they're about as wide as the bread. Top each pair with two overlapping slices of cheese.

When the oven's preheated, bake until the meatloaf is warmed through and the cheese has fully melted and, 4 to 6 minutes.

Slather the gravy mayo on one side of each piece of bread. Add a dollop of pepper jelly to one slice (a heaping 1 tablespoon per sandwich) and spread it as best you can. Top four pieces of the bread with some onion and the shrettuce. Use a spatula to perch the cheesy meatloaf slices on the shrettuce. Top with the pickles, sprinkle with the sesame seeds, and cover with the remaining bread slices. Eat.

TASTES-LIKE-THERE'S-GRAVY-IN-IT MAYO

Sure, you could use straight mayo for a meatloaf sandwich, but if you have drippings from your loaf, it seems crazy not to whisk them into your mayo. That's what we did—until the day we burned the meatloaf, so I whisked this together and couldn't tell the difference. Makes a generous ¾ cup

1 tablespoon awase miso

1 tablespoon Worcestershire sauce

¾ cup mayo (Duke's or bust)

Combine the miso and Worcestershire sauce in a medium bowl, stir until smooth, then add the mayo and stir well again.

It keeps in the fridge until the expiration date on your mayo.

6

Dishes For Meat

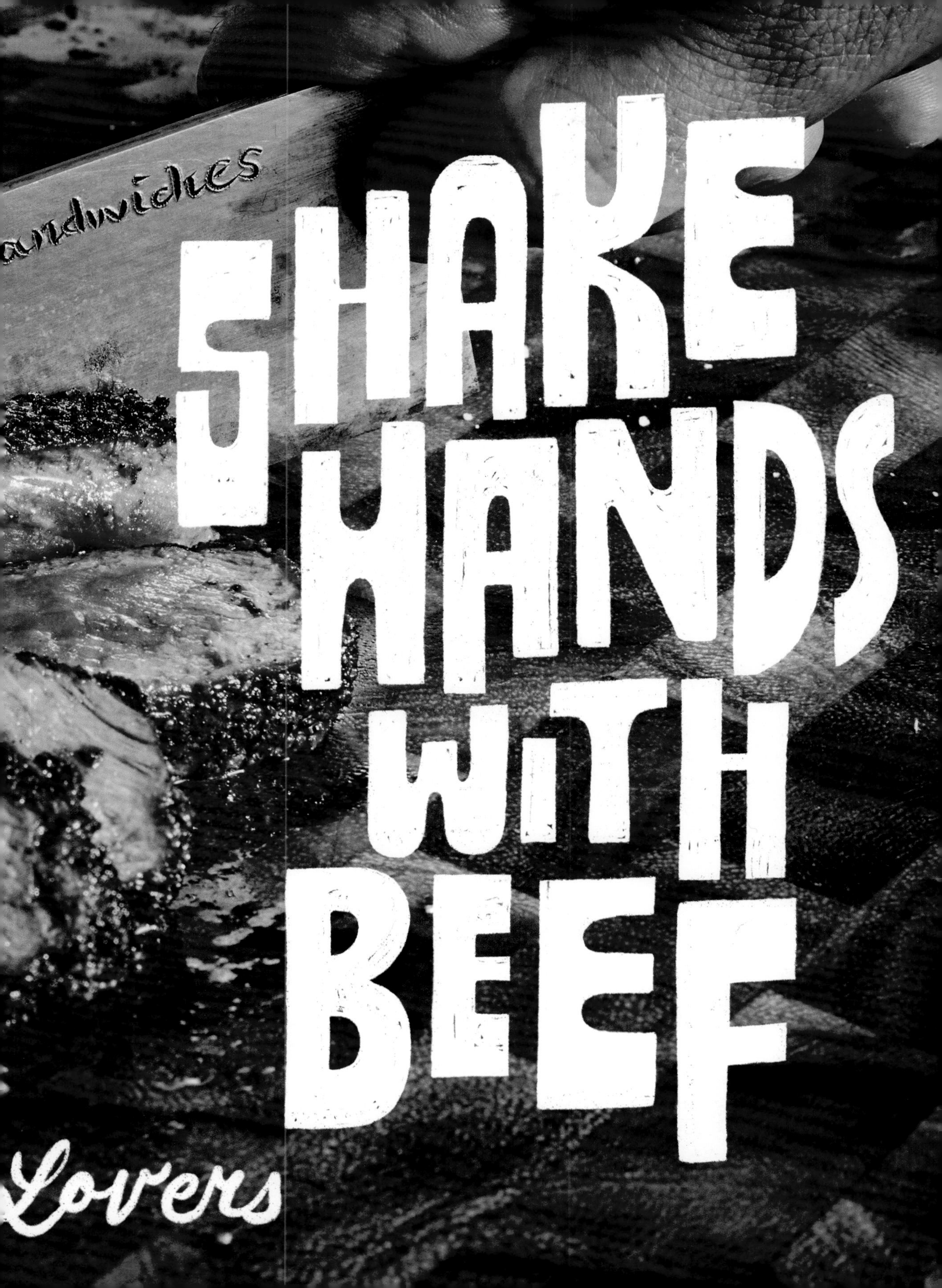
andwiches
SHAKE HANDS WITH BEEF
Lovers

CHICKEN POTPIES THAT FIT IN YOUR POCKET

Over the years we've stuffed a lot of fun inside store-bought discs of roti paratha to make our take on hand pies. But nothing—not collards, not braised lamb, not even the myriad flavors of Hot Pockets—hits me like this chicken potpie filling. It comforts me more than Stouffer's and Xanax, combined. Potpies made empanada-style up the flaky-crust-to-filling ratio and provide dunkability (preferably in a tarragon-buttermilk situation).

You can form these up to a day ahead and keep them in the fridge. You can also freeze some until they're solid and store in freezer bags until cravings strike, up to two months later. Then bake them from frozen—they'll take just a couple extra minutes.

Pro move: At the restaurant, we deep-fry 'em, but that's a hell of a task at home after all that cooking and filling. Still, if you want more crackle to your crust, get you a pot of oil and gun it to 350°F, but baking is no less a delight.

To make the filling: Get your oven to 375°F.

Spatchcock the chicken (if you don't know, google it). Season it all over with 1 tablespoon of the salt and 1 tablespoon of the pepper. Get 1 tablespoon of the oil hot in a Dutch oven over medium heat. Sear the chicken (if it won't fit, cut that sucker in half and sear in batches) on both sides until it looks like Kramer in that episode of *Seinfeld* when he butters himself and falls asleep in the sun. Throw the backbone in there, too, because why not.

Put the chicken on a plate, then cook the roughly chopped onion, carrot, and celery plus the garlic for a couple of minutes, scraping up any browned

bits. Add 1 cup water, scrape some more, then add the chicken bouillon and another 5 cups water. Add the bird, cover with a tight lid or foil, and cook in the oven for 1½ hours. It's done when you try to pick the chicken up by the leg and the leg comes off.

Meanwhile, cook the diced onion, carrot, and celery with the remaining 1 tablespoon oil in a medium skillet over medium-low heat until the onion is translucent. Scrape them into a large mixing bowl and set aside. Now get the chicken fat hot in that same skillet over medium-high heat, then sprinkle in the flour and immediately get whisking until the flour smell

continued

MAKES 15 OR 16

Filling

One 4- to 4½-pound whole chicken (preferably one that had hobbies)

1½ tablespoons kosher salt (Diamond Crystal or about half as much Morton), or more if you like

2 tablespoons freshly ground black pepper

2 tablespoons vegetable oil

2 large onions; 1 roughly chopped, 1 finely diced

2 large carrots; 1 roughly chopped, 1 finely diced

4 celery stalks; 2 roughly chopped, 2 finely diced

5 garlic cloves, roughly chopped

2 tablespoons granulated chicken bouillon (preferably Totole brand, see page 110; optional but optimal)

¼ cup rendered chicken fat (ideally) or unsalted butter

¼ cup all-purpose flour

3 tablespoons chopped thyme leaves

3 tablespoons chopped rosemary leaves

2 tablespoons Huy Fong Foods Sriracha

1 tablespoon Louisiana-style hot sauce

2 teaspoons sherry vinegar

dissipates and the resulting roux turns the barely golden color of a McDonald's french fry, 2 to 3 minutes. Scrape it into a little bowl and set aside.

When the chicken's done, move it to a plate and let it cool. Use a mesh skimmer or spider to scoop out and discard the solids in the Dutch oven, leaving the liquid behind. Bring to a boil over high heat, then lower the heat to simmer until the liquid is reduced to about 2 cups, 15 to 20 minutes. Whisk in 3 tablespoons of that roux (but keep the rest handy) plus the thyme and rosemary. Let it boil again and cook for a few minutes, until it's as thick as Texas queso. Whisk in more roux, if necessary. Set this gravy aside.

Ditch the skin from the cooled chicken (or treat your dog), then pick the meat into bite-size pieces and put it in the large mixing bowl with the reserved vegetables. Stir in the gravy, sriracha, hot sauce, sherry vinegar, and remaining ½ tablespoon salt and 1 tablespoon pepper. Add more salt until you're happy. Let the mixture chill in the fridge for an hour or so (up to 3 days). Filling the pies is easier when it's cooled down.

To assemble those pies: Take the roti paratha packages out of the freezer and let them thaw for 5 to 10 minutes, so they're pliable. You can separate them to speed this up. If they get too soft, pop them back in the freezer for a bit. For each potpie, scoop a slightly generous ⅓ cup of the filling in the center of a roti paratha. Gently fold the roti paratha over the filling so the edges touch, gently pinch them together with your fingers, and then use a fork to crimp the edges to seal the dough.

Get your oven to 375°F. Line a baking sheet with parchment paper or foil.

Put the pies on the baking sheet with an inch or so between them. In a small bowl, whisk the eggs with 2 tablespoons water until solid yellow. Brush or rub the mixture on the tops and edges of the pies, then liberally and evenly sprinkle with the chicken salt. Bake until they're ice-cream-cone brown and hot in the middle, 30 to 35 minutes.

Mix the buttermilk dressing and tarragon in a bowl. Dip the potpies. Eat them.

For the Pies

15 or 16 frozen roti paratha (see facing page)

2 eggs

Chicken Salt (page 231) or kosher salt

1 cup Big Zesty Buttermilk Dressing (page 226)

Two 2-ounce clamshells tarragon, finely chopped (about ½ cup)

ROTI PARATHA
*THE PREPARED DOUGH THAT'S NEVER NOT IN MY FREEZER

This doesn't refer to Indian roti or paratha, but rather a flaky, buttery flatbread born in India and modified by the Southeast Asian cooks who took it up. I read that. I'll admit to knowing very little about it, other than it takes tremendous skill to make and that I lack that skill tremendously. So I look to the frozen product, which is exceedingly delicious. I use it as the base for sorta sandwiches, as a bread for dipping in stuff, and wrapping savory hand pies. Over the years, more than one pastry chef has asked how we make the dough. In response, I disappear into the kitchen and emerge with a five-pack of the Spring Home brand for them to take home.

Look for it at many Asian and Indian super-markets. Look for "roti paratha," "roti canai," or "roti prata" on the label. If you're late to this party, like I am, having them in your freezer will be a huge win for your cooking.

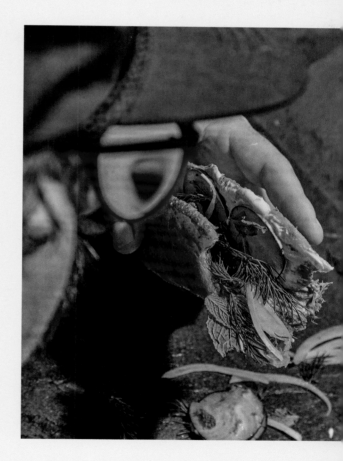

CORNER-STORE PORK RIND TACOS

A little while back, Turkey and the Wolf's chef de cuisine Nate put me on to a spot near the New Orleans airport serving chicharrón tacos, and now I hit up Chilangos Restaurant every time I'm near Louis Armstrong International. I live for the fried pork skins simmered to gooey, quivering softness in spicy, tangy salsa verde and spooned onto warm tortillas, but when this corner-store enthusiast makes them at home, I buy pork rinds and briefly toss them with the salsa so they're just warm and retain a little crunch in the middle. If you're afraid of the sog, which is kinda my favorite part, toss the pork rinds in just half a cup of the tomatillo salsa and reserve the rest for dunking your tacos.

MAKES 12

Salsa Verde

2 pounds tomatillos, husked and rinsed

1 small white onion, roughly chopped

2 serranos or jalapeños, stems removed

4 garlic cloves, peeled

2 tablespoons kosher salt (Diamond Crystal or about half as much Morton), or more if you like

1 bunch cilantro, trimmed and roughly chopped (about 1½ cups tightly packed)

1½ tablespoons grapeseed oil or vegetable oil

Tacos

12 corn tortillas (the best you can get)

Green Taco Sauce (page 138) or your favorite green hot sauce for serving

1 cup or so diced white onion

1 cup or so chopped cilantro

10 or so small lime wedges

6 cups (3 ounces) store-bought pork rinds or roughly crumbled chicharrón

To make the salsa: In a medium pot, combine the tomatillos, onion, serranos, garlic, salt, and enough water to submerge the ingredients (though they'll float, and that's OK). Bring it to a boil, then cook at a simmer, gently stirring occasionally, until the tomatillos are fully soft and pulpy but before they burst, 20 to 30 minutes.

Use a slotted spoon to move the contents of the pot to your blender, leaving the water behind, and puree until nice and smooth. Add the cilantro, then blend just until the cilantro flecks the salsa.

Get the oil hot in a heavy medium pot over high heat. Carefully pour in the salsa (it'll bubble, spit, and make fun noises), let it come to a boil, then cook, stirring frequently, until it thickens slightly, 1 to 2 minutes. Season with salt until you're happy.

Cover to keep it warm or let it cool and refrigerate in an airtight container for up to 5 days or freeze it for up to 3 months.

To assemble the tacos: Line a large bowl with a kitchen towel. Heat the tortillas on the open flame of a gas burner or in a hot cast-iron pan until you see small brown spots on both sides but they're still soft, not brittle. As they're ready, put them in the bowl, place another towel over them, and cover with a lid or plate.

When all the tortillas are ready, put the bowl on the table along with the taco sauce and a plate with the diced onion, chopped cilantro, and lime wedges.

Right before you're ready to serve, bring the salsa verde to a bare simmer and turn off the heat. Put the pork rinds in a large bowl, add 1 cup of the salsa, and toss until completely coated. Immediately bring them to the table with a spoon and tell your friends to make tacos with them and all the other stuff before the rinds lose their crunch. Serve the remaining tomatillo salsa on the side.

GREEN TACO SAUCE

The day I tried the sneaky-spicy green sauce at Chilangos Restaurant, out by Louis Armstrong Airport, I refilled the tiny paper cup it came in so many times that I think I ate a pint of it, all told. The next day, I started trying to make it myself, so I could eat (drink?) more. This version features many of the sauce's pleasures—an almost creamy texture from the oil, an awesome grassy heat from the chiles, and a sharpness that kicks in late, tempting you to take yet another hit. **Makes about 1 cup**

3 jalapeños

3 serranos (or another 3 jalapeños)

Kosher salt

1 garlic clove, peeled

2 tablespoons distilled white vinegar

½ cup grapeseed, canola, or another neutral oil

Put the jalapeños, serranos, and a handful of salt in a small pot and pour in enough water to cover the chiles by an inch or so (they'll float, and that's OK). Bring to a boil, then cook at a steady simmer, flipping the chiles occasionally, until they turn olive green and a few of them deflate or bust open, about 30 minutes.

Use a slotted spoon to move the chiles to your blender, discarding the water, and add the garlic, vinegar, and 1 teaspoon salt. With the blender running on high speed, slowly drizzle in the oil. Season with more salt until you're happy.

It keeps in an airtight container in the fridge for up to 1 week.

FRIED CHICKEN SKINS AND DEVILED EGGS

Straight-up deviled eggs here, super-easy to make and nice and bright from lemon, mustard, and hot sauce. Can't beat that, except with some salty crunch. For that, I look to the other star of my Southern picnic memories: fried chicken. But just the skin, which after some diligent fat-scraping, a quick blanch, a simple dredge, and a bath in hot oil steals the show. Let the record show they're your best option, but also that I often get lazy and eat my eggs with corner-store pork rinds or even crunchy skin pulled right off some Popeyes, if I have either on hand.

To make the chicken skins: Put the chicken skin bumpy-side down on a cutting board. Working with one piece at a time, use a spoon or butter knife to scrape off as much of the opaque layer of fat as you can (do it pretty gently, so you don't tear the skin). You're trying for pieces of more or less translucent skin—the more fat you're able to scrape off, the crispier the end result will be. If you leave some little pockets of fat, though, that's not the end of the world.

Put the scraped skins in a small pot, add enough water to cover them, and bring it to a boil. Turn off the heat, let them hang out for 15 minutes, then drain well. Let them cool, then tear or chop them into roughly 2-inch pieces.

Get 2 inches of oil to 350°F in a large pot over medium-high heat. Meanwhile, stir together the flour, cornmeal, bread crumbs, paprika, onion powder, garlic powder, celery salt, and cayenne in a medium mixing bowl. Line a large plate with paper towels and put it near the pot.

When the oil's ready, add the chicken skins to the flour mixture and toss until they're well coated. Working in batches if necessary so you don't crowd the oil, carefully fry the skins—stand back at first, because they tend to pop and spit early on—until they're fried-chicken brown and crispy, about 4 minutes per batch. Give them a stir occasionally so the skins don't stick together.

Use a skimmer or slotted spoon to move them to the paper towel–lined plate, then season immediately and generously with salt. They'll stay crispy for a while. Cooled, they keep in an airtight container at room temp for a few days.

To make the deviled eggs: Pop the yolks out of the whites and put in a food processor. Reserve all but four of the white halves, which you could eat, I guess, or feed to your dog. If you're feeling fancy, rinse the whites under cold water to remove any lingering yolk, then pat dry.

continued

Fried Chicken Skins

8 ounces chicken skin (see "A Note on Those Chicken Skins")

Vegetable oil for deep-frying (about 2 quarts)

½ cup plus 2 tablespoons all-purpose flour

½ cup cornmeal, preferably coarse but fine works, too

½ cup panko bread crumbs, finely ground

2¼ teaspoons smoked paprika

1½ teaspoons onion powder

1½ teaspoons garlic powder

1½ teaspoons celery salt

½ teaspoon cayenne pepper

Kosher salt

Deviled Eggs

12 hard-boiled eggs, peeled and halved lengthwise

¼ cup mayo (Duke's or bust)

1 tablespoon plus 1 teaspoon Louisiana-style hot sauce, or more if you like

Heaping 2 teaspoons Dijon mustard

2 tablespoons lemon juice

1½ teaspoons kosher salt (Diamond Crystal or about half as much Morton)

Freshly ground black pepper

Torn dill for garnish

Add the mayo, hot sauce, mustard, lemon juice, and the salt to a food processor and pulse just until well mixed, smooth, and slightly fluffy. Don't over-process, or it'll get liquidy.

Put the egg whites on a platter. Scoop the yolk mixture into a small resealable bag, guide it toward a corner, and snip off the corner with scissors. Pipe the mixture evenly into the whites. Garnish them with the chicken skins, black pepper, dill, and, if you want, a little more hot sauce before serving.

A NOTE ON THOSE CHICKEN SKINS

First, see if a friendly butcher will sell you half a pound of chicken skin. If that fails, no sweat. Buy two chickens, then remove the skin with a knife or scissors. Don't go nuts trying to get every piece. You'll get plenty from the breast, back, and thighs. The nude birds you'll have left are great for poaching. Two birds will give you about twelve ounces of skin.

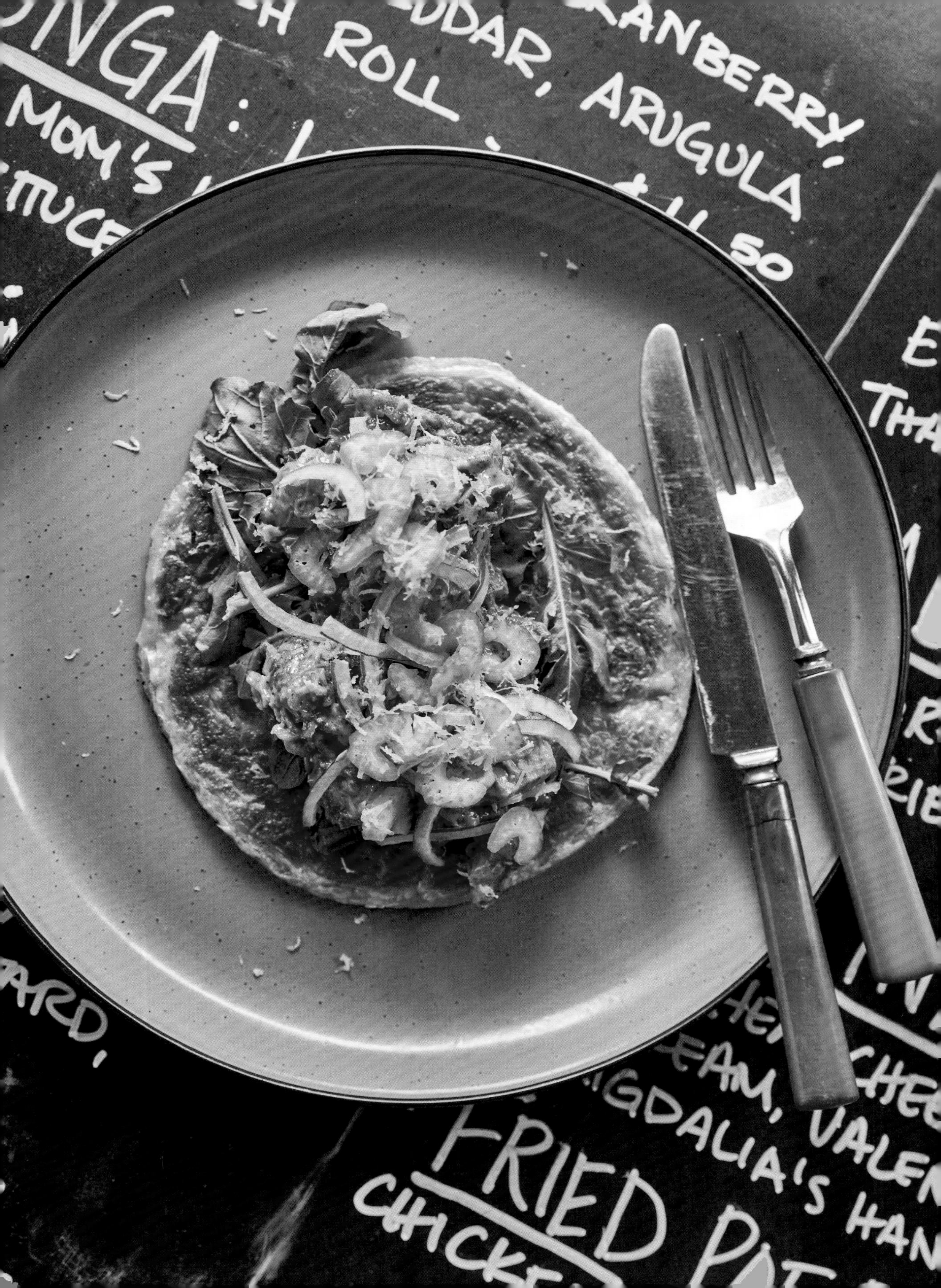
ROLL
ARUGULA
MOM'S
FRIED

SPICY FRIED CHICKEN SALAD ON ROTI PARATHA

This one reads pretty straightforward compared to the rest of the madness in these pages, but it's such a dang delight. It came to be when the crew and I were musing about the extreme awesomeness of chicken salad on a croissant. Next thing you know, we're wrapping flaky, crackly, buttery roti paratha around fried chicken inundated with mayo and spiking the mixture with tons of lemon, some spices, and fresh, crisp greenery. Fried chicken has never tasted so refreshing. (It still ain't good for you.)

It's extra good with the fried chicken thighs from Nate's Spicy Fried Chicken Sandwich, because the awesome craggy crust from that Michael Solomonov–inspired version keeps some of its crunch. Still, any surplus will do, including spicy Popeyes. As long as you don't skip the spicy chicken spices, you can nail the flavors here. Any flatbread would technically work. Croissants, too.

MAKES 6

4 spicy fried chicken thighs (see page 197)

A little less than 1 cup mayo (Duke's or bust)

4 tablespoons unsalted butter, room-temp so it's mayo-soft

6 frozen roti paratha (see page 135) or another tasty flatbread

Handful of arugula

Some very thinly sliced red onion

Some thinly sliced celery

3 juicy lemons, for zesting and juicing

1½ teaspoons Nate's Spicy Chicken Spices (page 230)

Cut the fried chicken into ¾-inch-ish cubes and put them in a medium bowl. Add the mayo and stir until the chicken is coated and glorious.

Get a nonstick pan hot over medium heat. Spread a little of the softened butter on both sides of the frozen roti paratha and cook them, one at a time, in the pan until they're golden brown on both sides and they begin to puff up, about 2 minutes per side.

Arrange the arugula along the center of each roti paratha, put your mayo-chicken goodness on the arugula, then the onion and celery on top of the chicken. Next, Microplane to zest half a lemon onto each, then squeeze half a lemon's worth of juice onto each one as well. Finally, sprinkle on the chicken spices and eat.

SLOW-COOKED LAMB NECKS WITH FIXINGS ON ROTI PARATHA

I love me some lamb neck! After you brown and braise it, this affordable cut gives you super-tender, super-lamby lamb. Once it's cooked, we apply our go-to braised-meat move, reducing the cooking liquid to an intensified gravy to sauce it up. Lamb loves spices and chiles, so whip up my spiced chile paste or buy some harissa; no matter which you choose, it makes a warm hug of a meal on rice, couscous, or flaky roti paratha.

Lemony-ass yogurt cools and brightens things up, though when I announced this dish, hyphen-free, on Instagram, my buddy Bart Bell commented that he'd take his "ass yogurt" on the side. Still makes me smile.

To make the lamb: Get your oven to 325°F.

Get the oil hot in a wide, oven-proof pot (like a 5- to 6-quart Dutch oven) over medium-high heat. Pat the lamb necks dry, generously salt and pepper them, then brown them, turning once, about 10 minutes.

Move the necks to a plate, leaving the fat behind, then add the onion, carrots, celery, garlic, thyme, and bay leaves to the pot and cook, stirring occasionally, until the vegetables have softened and browned a bit, about 15 minutes. Add the tomato paste and stir constantly until it turns a shade or two darker, about 1 minute. Add the sherry vinegar, let it bubble, and scrape up any browned bits stuck to the pot.

Return the browned necks to the pot with enough water to come three-fourths or so up the sides of the necks. Bring to a simmer, cover, and then cook in the oven until the meat is super-tender, 3 to 3½ hours. Let it cool, uncovered, for about 30 minutes. Move the necks to a plate so they can fully cool.

Strain the liquid into a heatproof cup, pressing on the vegetables. (Save them for another day, because they're still real good.) Skim off the fat (it's way easier when it's cooled completely, but if you're antsy, spoon it off as best you can).

Pick the meat from the necks, discarding the bones, then combine it in a pot with the chile paste and strained liquid. (Cooled and refrigerated, it'll keep for up to 5 days.) Reheat gently, then season with salt until you're happy and cover to keep warm.

To assemble the dish: Get a non-stick pan hot over medium heat. Spread a little softened butter on both sides of the frozen roti

continued

MAKES 6

Lamb

3 tablespoons canola oil or vegetable oil

5 to 6 pounds whole lamb necks (about 2) or shanks (about 4)

Kosher salt

Freshly ground black pepper

1 white onion, roughly chopped

2 carrots, roughly chopped

2 celery stalks, roughly chopped

8 garlic cloves, peeled

2 tablespoons thyme leaves

3 bay leaves

¼ cup tomato paste

¼ cup sherry vinegar

½ cup Spiced Chile Paste (page 146) or store-bought harissa

For the dish

4 tablespoons unsalted butter, room-temp so it's mayo-soft

6 frozen roti paratha (see page 135) or another tasty flatbread

1 cup whole-milk Greek yogurt

1 teaspoon kosher salt (Diamond Crystal or about half as much Morton), or more if you like

paratha and cook them, one at a time, in the pan until they're golden brown on both sides and they begin to puff up, about 2 minutes per side. Put them on a plate.

Combine the yogurt and salt in a serving bowl. Zest one of the lemons into the bowl, then halve the lemon and squeeze in about 1 tablespoon juice. Stir well and add more salt and lemon juice until you're happy. Cut the remaining lemon into wedges.

Put the lamb, cucumber, onion, dill, mint, and lemon wedges out on the table and let your friends choose their own adventure.

2 juicy lemons

1 large cucumber, thinly sliced

Some very thinly sliced white onion

Handful of dill sprigs

Small handful of mint leaves

SPICED CHILE PASTE

This is what happens when a know-nothing attempts to make something like harissa through a bit of googling, trial and error, and maybe a little corner cutting. Don't get me wrong, I love this stuff, which is just the thing for our lamb neck roti. If you're using it for another purpose, you might cut back a little on the caraway. You could also buy real harissa from the store. Makes a generous 1 cup

Bring a small pot of water to a boil. Put the chiles in a medium heatproof bowl, pour on the boiling water, and let the chiles soften, about 30 minutes.

Meanwhile, toast the caraway, coriander, and cumin seeds in a small skillet over medium-low heat, swirling occasionally, until they smell really good, about 2 minutes. Let them cool and grind them to a powder in a

spice grinder or with a mortar and pestle.

Drain the chiles, reserving ½ cup of the soaking liquid. Combine the chiles, ground spices, garlic, oil, hot sauce, sriracha, and vinegar in your blender and blend until smooth, gradually adding some of the reserved soaking liquid to help it blend.

It keeps in the fridge for up to 2 months.

8 dried guajillo chiles (about 2 ounces), stemmed, slit open, and seeded

1 tablespoon caraway seeds

1 tablespoon coriander seeds

1 tablespoon cumin seeds

2 garlic cloves, peeled

2 tablespoons canola oil

2 tablespoons Louisiana-style hot sauce

½ tablespoon Huy Fong Foods Sriracha

½ teaspoon sherry vinegar

HOG'S HEAD CHEESE

My first encounter with hog's head cheese was at a party in New Orleans, where some kind gentleman had shown up with Club Crackers, Creole mustard, and a jiggly, sliceable loaf of cooked pork head purchased from some South Louisiana roadside butcher shop or boudin joint. It ruled.

But it wasn't until I dropped a chunk that we had kicking around at the restaurant into a pot of family-meal stew when my eyes opened to the jellied meat's versatility in hot preparations. Nowadays we turn it into tacos (see page 154), melt it into rice (see page 153), and toss it into collards (see page 157). I like to throw some in a pan with Velveeta and Ro*tel and eat that off saltines or chips. You can totally buy it! Spots like The Best Stop Supermarket and Billy's Boudin and Cracklin ship it, but you should probably make it at least once before you leave this world.

P.S. Check out the Hog's Head Cheese Itinerary on page 150.

To simmer that head: In a gigantic (6- to 8-gallon), heavy stockpot set over two stove-top burners, combine the pig's head (snout up), garlic, bay leaves, celery, onions, carrot, Creole seasoning, garlic powder, onion powder, and chile flakes. Pour in enough water (say, 4 gallons) to more or less submerge the head.

Turn the two burners to high and let the water come to a boil, about 1½ hours. Cover, lower the heat to maintain a gentle simmer, and cook, topping off with more water as necessary to keep the head submerged, until the meat is fall-apart tender, 7 to 8 hours. Turn off the heat. You might want to let it cool a bit.

Set out a large heatproof mixing bowl, and set a large chinois over a large pot. Use sturdy tongs to remove the head and then start picking off those tender pieces of meat, snout, skin, ears—everything that's not bone, hard cartilage, or teeth—and move it to the mixing bowl. Occasionally take a breather and start ladling the liquid through the strainer into the pot. When you've ladled in enough liquid so you can comfortably lift the heavy pot, you can speed things up by carefully pouring the liquid through the strainer. If you discover any new tender pig bits while you strain, add them to the mixing bowl. Otherwise, discard all the remaining solids—spices, vegetables, and hard stuff.

Put the hog's head goodies in the fridge, but not the shit ton of porky liquid.

continued

MAKES 1 GALLON

For Simmering the Head

1 whole pig's head
(15 to 20 pounds),
ears, jowls, and all

5 garlic cloves, peeled

5 dried or fresh bay leaves

4 celery stalks, halved

2 white onions, halved
and peeled

1 large carrot, peeled

¼ cup plus 2 tablespoons
Zatarain's Creole Seasoning

3 tablespoons
garlic powder

3 tablespoons
onion powder

2 tablespoons gochugaru
(Korean chile flakes) or
other red chile flakes

Head Cheese

3 celery stalks, halved

1 large carrot, peeled

1 white onion, halved
and peeled

½ cup Zatarain's
Creole Mustard

¼ cup plus 2 tablespoons
Huy Fong Foods Sriracha,
or more if you like

¼ cup Louisiana-style hot
sauce, or more if you like

3 tablespoons freshly
ground black pepper

3 tablespoons gochugaru
(Korean chile flakes) or
other red chile flakes

3 tablespoons
Worcestershire sauce

Kosher salt

To make the head cheese: Skim the fat from the surface of the liquid as best you can, then crank the heat so it boils. Lower the heat to simmer vigorously, stirring every 30 minutes or so and scraping the bottom of the pot occasionally during the last hour to prevent burning, until it has reduced to roughly 4 cups of very viscous liquid, 6 to 7 hours.

Meanwhile, boil a big pot of pretty salty water and make a big bowl of icy water. We make like we're fancy and brunoise the next round of celery, carrot, and onion, but feel free to pulse them in a food processor until they're in ¼- to ⅛-inch pieces. Add the chopped vegetables to the pot and cook until they're tender with a slight crunch, 30 seconds to 1 minute. Use a mesh strainer to get them in the icy water, let them cool, then drain well.

Once the porky liquid is ready, pour it into the bowl with the hog's head goodies. Stir in the chopped vegetables, mustard, sriracha, hot sauce, pepper, chile flakes, Worcestershire sauce, and 2 tablespoons salt. Give it a taste and gradually add more salt, sriracha, and hot sauce, if you want.

Use some hot (after all that, you deserve a snack) and let the rest cool. Stick it in a bunch of airtight containers or resealable bags. Store it in the fridge for up to 1 week or in the freezer for up to 6 months.

HOG'S HEAD CHEESE ITINERARY

This one is going to be a bit of a project. You have to procure that pork dome, cook it for forever with spices and aromatics, pick all that meat, reduce all that liquid to a rich gloss, then mix it all back together. You might have a moment while you're panning the liquid for stray teeth or cursing at the friend who's helping you tong a skull out of a steamy pot of stock, when you ask what you've gotten yourself into. But head cheese is cool, and you're welcome. Plus, it's mostly hands-off simmering. And that before-and-after selfie with the pig head and then the fully excavated brain bone is guaranteed Instagram gold.

Once you make head cheese, you've got a shit ton of it to give to friends, to freeze for future treats, and to use right away.

What you need

If you're going do this, make your life easy by getting a hold of:

1. a giant stockpot (at least 6 gallons)

2. a big-ass bucket, Cambro container, or enough assorted mixing bowls and pots to hold several gallons of strained liquid

3. a large chinois (one of those conical strainer dealies)

4. some deli containers or resealable bags (since it makes 16 cups)

5. a cooler full of ice, if you're breaking the process into two days (see facing page)

Note that a crawfish burner speeds up the process considerably.

WHEN DO I START THE ADVENTURE THAT IS MAKING HOG'S HEAD CHEESE?

Stick to this schedule and you can technically crank it out in a day.

7 a.m. Wake up, but don't even brush your teeth yet. Get the head and aromatics in the pot, set it over high heat, and go back to bed for an hour and a half. Should be boiling by then.

8:30 a.m. Tweak the heat so you've got a gentle simmer and let that head cook. Read a book.

4 p.m. Turn off the heat, let the head and liquid cool a bit, get picking and straining.

5 p.m. Start reducing the liquid, blanch those vegetables, then do more of your thing.

11 p.m. Mix everything together, let it cool, pack it away, and you're done.

For a more relaxed hog's head cheese–making schedule, break it up into two days. First, clear some space in your fridge for the meat and the liquid. After you pick that head meat and strain the liquid, let them cool (put the pot that the liquid's in into a cooler full of ice to speed this up) and store them in the fridge until you're ready to resume the next day. Before pouring the hot reduced liquid over the meat, break up the meat a bit, which, thanks to all the pork head's collagen, will take more strength than you expect.

HOG'S HEAD CHEESE RICE

This advice came from my friend Mandi Bordelon, from Rayne, Louisiana, and I'm glad I took it. A while back, she was serving at a restaurant where I was cooking. She saw me working on a dish with a fresh batch of head cheese and said something along the lines of, "You should mix it with some rice." I did, and it was a revelation. Easier than jambalaya and porkier than dirty rice (and as tasty as both), this dish is mega easy if you've got head cheese on hand.

Easy pickled peppers along with lemon juice and hot sauce keep things on the bright side of the road. I have some advice, too: Really go crazy with that pepper grinder for this one. To make it looks kinda '70s, like I did in the photo, pack it into a bowl and then flip onto a plate.

SERVES 2 TO 4

2 cups (about 1 pound) Hog's Head Cheese, homemade (page 147) or from the store

⅔ cup drained Pickled Sweet Peppers, homemade (recipe follows) or jarred

2 tablespoons unsalted butter

3 cups cooked white rice

2 tablespoons Louisiana-style hot sauce, plus the bottle for the table

1 juicy lemon

Kosher salt

Freshly ground black pepper

Heat the head cheese, pickled peppers, and butter in a skillet over medium heat, stirring occasionally, until the head cheese melts into hot, thick braise-y gravy, about 5 minutes.

Add the rice and hot sauce and cook, stirring occasionally, until the rice is warm and totally coated by the warm head cheese and it's all one big party, about 5 minutes more.

Stir in the juice of the lemon and give it a taste. You'll probably want to add some salt, up to 2 teaspoons, but go gradually, because head cheeses will vary a bit in saltiness. Crank on some pepper—go wild, because black pepper really makes this dish—and you're good to go. Serve it up with the hot sauce bottle on the table.

PICKLED SWEET PEPPERS

Pickling like this takes just minutes. The brine and method work on thinly sliced onions and carrots, too. Makes about ¾ cup

1½ cups thinly sliced mini sweet peppers (6 or 7)

1 cup unseasoned rice vinegar

½ cup white sugar

2½ tablespoons kosher salt (Diamond Crystal or about half as much Morton), or more if you like

Put the sweet peppers in a medium heatproof container. In a small pot, combine the vinegar, sugar, and salt; set it over high heat; and bring it to a simmer, stirring occasionally to help the sugar and salt dissolve. When it simmers, immediately pour the hot liquid over the peppers. Let cool fully.

The peppers are ready to go now, though they're even better after a day of pickling. Toss 'em in the fridge and keep them for up to 1 month.

HOG'S HEAD CHEESE TACOS

One night during the blissfully wild first month that Turkey and the Wolf was open, we were making each other snacks before service. We passed a plate of American cheese melted over one of Migdalia's fine tortillas, topped with a tidy mess of warm head cheese, and crowned with our holy trinity of impromptu Tex-Mex—sour cream, shrettuce, and hot sauce. After we'd all taken bites, we locked eyes and nodded. Sometimes the simplest dishes take the most testing to get right, but not this one. The next day, it was on the menu.

Don't sleep on the Strippies—they bring off-brand-Doritos-esque spice and texture.

MAKES 12

2 cups (about 1 pound) Hog's Head Cheese, homemade (page 147) or from the store

12 corn tortillas (the best you can get)

12 thin slices American cheese

⅔ cup sour cream

1 bottle of your go-to Mexican hot sauce (mine's Valentina)

3 cups shrettuce (see page 229)

1 to 2 jalapeños, thinly sliced into rings

Strippies (facing page) for serving

Set your oven to real low, just so it's warm inside.

Melt the head cheese in a skillet over medium-low heat, stirring occasionally, to a hot, thick braise-y gravy, 3 to 5 minutes. Turn off the heat and cover to keep it warm.

Meanwhile, set a heavy skillet (cast iron works great) over medium-high heat and let it get nice and hot—say, for about 2 minutes. Add a tortilla (or two, if the skillet is wide enough) and let it hang out until it starts to get a nice toasty smell (a good tortilla will even puff a bit), 2 minutes. Flip the tortilla, immediately add a slice of cheese, and let it hang out for 1 minute, so the cheese gets melty.

Move the tortilla to a baking sheet, stick it in the warm oven, and repeat this process with the remaining tortillas and cheese slices. When all the tortillas are ready, serve them with a bowl of the melted head cheese and the rest of the fixings.

Now you can go wild, but here's how I make each one: I spoon some warm head cheese (like, 2 tablespoons or so) down the middle of each tortilla. Then I hit each one with a dollop of sour cream (2 teaspoons should do it), a nice splash of hot sauce (like, 1 teaspoon), a small hand-ful (¼ cup or so) of shrettuce, as many jalapeño slices as I can handle, and a generous pinch (2-ish tablespoons) of strippies. Eat ASAP!

STRIPPIES

No fryer necessary for these Doritos-like toppers for tacos (facing page), taco salads, or even non-taco meals that could benefit from some crunch and spice. Makes about 1¾ cups

Get your oven to 450°F.

Stack the tortillas and cut them into ¼-inch strips. Put them in a mixing bowl, drizzle in the oil, and toss until they're well coated. Spread them in a single layer on a baking sheet, and into the oven they go for 6 to 8 minutes, until they're brown like a graham cracker and crunchy like chips. Rotate the pan halfway through, so they cook evenly.

While they bake, line a plate or tray with paper towels, and mix together the taco seasoning and salt in a small bowl. When the strippies are done, immediately sprinkle with the taco seasoning–salt mixture and use tongs to toss them so they get good and coated. Move them to the plate or tray, to drain any excess oil.

Cooled, they keep in an airtight container at room temp until they get stale, which, if you're lucky, won't be for a couple weeks.

Five 6-inch corn tortillas, or six 5-inch ones

¼ cup vegetable oil

2 tablespoons taco seasoning mix (preferably McCormick)

½ teaspoon kosher salt (Diamond Crystal or about half as much Morton)

HOG'S HEAD CHEESE COLLARDS

Here's one that takes a bunch of work if you've got nothing to start with but is basically zero work if you've already got head cheese and stewed collard greens in the fridge. On multiple occasions, I've served it alongside some dish I put a lot of thought and work into, and people generally liked the hog's head cheese collards best.

SERVES 4 TO 6

3 cups Scotty's Good-with-Everything Collard Greens (page 178), plus a little pot likker

1½ cups (12 ounces) Hog's Head Cheese, homemade (page 147) or from the store

1 teaspoon Zatarain's Creole Seasoning

1 tablespoon Louisiana-style hot sauce

Put those collards, that head cheese, and the Creole seasoning and hot sauce in a medium pot and mix them up. Get it all good and hot over medium heat, 5 to 10 minutes.

Taste it. If you're using store-bought head cheese, you'll probably want to go harder on that Creole seasoning and hot sauce. Once it's good, go at it.

HOW TO STEAK

When I want some steak, I go to La Boca, Adolfo Garcia's Argentine steakhouse in New Orleans. If I can't go there, I make my own. Here's how.

I get two good, thick 1-pound boneless strip steaks and season them with so much salt and pepper—like 3 tablespoons kosher salt (Diamond Crystal or about half as much Morton) and 2 tablespoons freshly ground black pepper—that you think to yourself, "That's way too much salt and pepper." It's not. It makes a crackly crust and ensures each slice is seasoned real nice.

Then get a couple of tablespoons of vegetable oil smoking hot in a cast-iron skillet (big enough to hold the two steaks with plenty of space in between) over high heat. Add the steaks, lower the heat to medium, and let that first side get a nice brown crust, 1 to 2 minutes.

Flip the steaks and cook, flipping them every minute or so and occasionally standing them on their sides, until they develop a dark brown crust on all sides and an instant-read thermometer inserted into their centers registers 120°F (after resting, they'll be medium-rare), about 10 minutes total. Move them to a cutting board to rest for 10 minutes or so.

Now, slice the steaks against the grain into ¼- to ½-inch-thick slices, and move them to a platter along with any juicy stuff. Sprinkle on some flaky sea salt and seriously consider serving it with both bright, herby Verdant Blender Sauce (page 216) and salty, zippy Grocery-Store Tonnato Sauce (page 161).

GROCERY-STORE TONNATO SAUCE

Turns out all the dope tuna sandwiches I ate when I was little was nature preparing me to love tonnato as an adult. That creamy Northern Italian sauce isn't just good with braised, chilled, thinly sliced cold veal (its classic partner); it's good with everything. And so is this riff made with some cherry peppers for extra zip. I like it even better the next day, when it thickens a bit and the flavors come together.

MAKES ABOUT 1½ CUPS

One 5-ounce can oil-packed tuna, drained

2 tablespoons extra-virgin olive oil

8 slices pickled hot cherry peppers (from a jar)

2 oil-packed anchovy fillets, drained

Heaping 2 teaspoons capers, drained

1 teaspoon kosher salt (Diamond Crystal or about half as much Morton), or more if you like

¼ teaspoon cayenne pepper

2 juicy lemons, halved

½ cup mayo (Duke's or bust)

Combine the tuna, oil, cherry peppers, anchovies, capers, salt, and cayenne in a blender or food processor; squeeze in three of the lemon halves; then blend on high speed until it's smooth, about 1 minute. Scrape into a mixing bowl and stir in the mayo. Season with more salt and lemon juice.

It keeps in the fridge for up to 1 week.

SIDE
HUSTLE

7 FIXINGS

MOM'S FAMOUS BURNT TOMATOES

For years, I used to host a huge Thanksgiving dinner in New Orleans with my buddy Via. As a young cook with lots to prove to my friends and family, I always made two giant turkeys and a dozen sides. My mom would make just one accompaniment— burnt tomatoes, a dish she learned from my old man's mom, Ann Hereford. And guess which dish was always the talk of the meal?

What, at a glance, seems like an odd, overcooked casserole is actually a masterstroke: stacks of buttery, sugar-sprinkled, lightly charred pan-fried tomatoes blasted in the oven until they melt into red-brown lava that's sweet and tart and rich and incredible. It's still my favorite thing on any table.

SERVES 10 TO 12

6 tablespoons unsalted butter

3 cups all-purpose flour

3 tablespoons kosher salt (Diamond Crystal or about half as much Morton)

2 tablespoons freshly ground black pepper

1 tablespoon white sugar

Lots of canola oil (4 to 6 cups)

6 pounds large tomatoes (10 to 12), cored and cut into ½-inch round slices

Get ready because these babies take about an hour to fry and stack and otherwise prep for baking.

Rub about 1 tablespoon of the butter on the bottom and up the sides of a 9 by 13-inch baking dish. Dice the rest of the butter into pea-size pieces. In a medium mixing bowl, stir together the flour, 1 tablespoon of the salt, and 1 tablespoon of the pepper. In a small mixing bowl, stir together the remaining 2 tablespoons salt, 1 tablespoon pepper, and the sugar.

Pour 1 inch of oil into a deep cast-iron skillet and get it shimmering over medium-high heat. Working in batches to avoid crowding the oil, add four or five tomato slices to the flour mixture, toss to coat them well, and fry them in a single layer, flipping once, until they get brown on both sides and real soft, about 6 minutes. (If they take much time longer, turn up the heat for the next round.)

As the tomatoes are done, use a slotted spatula to drain off as much oil as you can (try rapping on the edge of the pot) and then move the tomatoes to the buttered baking dish in a single layer. Keep frying and lining that baking dish until the bottom's covered, then add about half the diced butter (a piece or two per slice) and evenly sprinkle on about a third of the sugar mixture.

Meanwhile, get your oven to 375°F.

Keep frying, adding a little more oil if necessary to maintain the depth and not stressing if the oil gets real dark. Continue to move the slices to the baking dish to make neat-ish stacks. Once you've finished the second layer of tomatoes, add the remaining butter and another even sprinkle of a third of the sugar mixture. You should have enough tomatoes to make stacks of three (any extras can become fours).

continued

Once you've finished frying and stacking the remaining tomatoes, sprinkle with the remaining sugar mixture.

Move the baking dish to the oven and cook, uncovered, until the tomatoes have shrunk, leaked oil, and turned deep brown and nearly black in spots, about 2 hours, though my mom claims it's impossible to overcook. At this point, it's lava-hot, so let it cool for 10 minutes, then serve your friends a stack.

Leftovers keep in the fridge for up to 5 days. Reheat them, covered, in a 350°F oven until hot.

BUTTERMILK MASHED POTATOES

Hell yeah we got a mashed potatoes recipe in this book! These take me back to my grandmother Anne's table, though rumor has it hers were so good because she added a pinch of sugar, and I could never figure out how that worked. Instead, the key to these is sufficiently salting the boiling water so the taters are seasoned to their core before you mash them and hit them with just the right levels of dairy overkill. If you can, time it so you can make them and eat them right away. They're the best like that.

SERVES 6 TO 8

⅔ cup sour cream

½ cup well-shaken buttermilk

4½ pounds (about 4 large) russet potatoes, peeled and cut into 1-inch pieces

⅔ cup kosher salt (Diamond Crystal or about half as much Morton)

2 sticks (16 tablespoons) unsalted butter

⅔ cup heavy cream

Let the sour cream and buttermilk hang out at room temp while you cook the potatoes, so they lose their chill.

Combine the potatoes, salt, and 12 cups water in a medium pot, then get it boiling. Lower the heat and gently simmer the potatoes until a fork slides into them real easy, about 15 minutes.

Meanwhile, get the butter and heavy cream warm in a small pot over medium heat so all the butter melts. Cover and keep warm off the heat.

When the potatoes are ready, drain them well, then put them back in the pot. Add the butter mixture, give it a good stir, then add the sour cream and buttermilk and get to mixing and mashing. Keep at it just until it's well mixed and smooth-ish; too much mixing and mashing will give you gummy potatoes

Serve them good and hot.

MY BEST ATTEMPT AT ANNE HEREFORD'S APPLE FRITTERS

I have no more vivid memory of my grandmother Anne than sitting around her huge dining room table—or if the cousins were in town, at the kids' table with a lazy Susan—eating fried chicken, corn pudding, and apple fritters. And that's right: Those apple fritters ain't dessert. They're dinner, even though the slices get dunked in a rustic batter made with enough sugar to give them an incredible brown, craggy, chewy crust. I had forgotten about that chew, so when I rediscovered it during many rounds of working on this recipe—one of only a few missing from my mega collection of Anne's old clippings and cooking scribbles—I knew I'd cracked it.

MAKES ABOUT 20 FRITTERS (3 OR 4 PER PERSON)

2 cups all-purpose flour

2 cups well-shaken buttermilk

1 cup Jiffy Corn Muffin Mix

6 tablespoons white sugar

½ teaspoon ground cinnamon

½ teaspoon freshly ground black pepper

2 large sweet-tart apples, like Honeycrisp or Pink Lady

1 tablespoon kosher salt (Diamond Crystal or about half as much Morton)

Vegetable oil for deep-frying (about 2 quarts)

Grab three medium mixing bowls and set them in a row. In the first, put 1 cup of the flour. In the second, put the buttermilk. In the third, combine the Jiffy mix, the remaining 1 cup flour, 5 tablespoons of the sugar, the cinnamon, and pepper and stir really well.

Cut the top and bottom off the apples, then cut through the core into thin, round slices (about ⅛ inch thick), flicking out any seeds. You want 20 or so slices. In a small bowl, mix the remaining 1 tablespoon sugar with the salt and set it aside.

Bring 2 inches of oil to 350°F in a large heavy pot over medium-high heat. Line a baking sheet with a wire rack or paper towels.

Working in four or five batches, toss the apple slices in the flour to coat well, shaking off the excess. Submerge the floured apple slices in the buttermilk until completely coated, letting any excess drip back into the bowl. Then toss them with the Jiffy mixture to coat in a thin layer. Move them to a second baking sheet as they're done. Now, they're ready to swim.

Fry the apple slices in four batches to avoid crowding in the oil, flipping them over once, until they're dark golden brown, about 5 minutes. When they're done, use a slotted spoon or mesh strainer to move them to the prepared baking sheet in a single layer and right away sprinkle with the sugar mixture on both sides.

When they're cool enough to eat, you just might be cool enough to eat them.

MASON'S DANKSGIVING DAY PUREE

I make this stuff every year, because I like saying "Mason's Danksgiving Day Puree," but I also do it because it's delicious. The apples lend acidity to balance an otherwise classically rich Turkey Day side dish, and the spices make it delightfully seasonal.

SERVES 6 TO 8

3¾ pounds (about 5) sweet potatoes

2 large medium-tart apples, like Pink Lady or Honeycrisp

1 stick (8 tablespoons) plus 1 tablespoon unsalted butter

½ teaspoon ground cinnamon

½ teaspoon ground allspice

½ teaspoon ground cloves

½ cup heavy cream

3 tablespoons maple syrup

Heaping 1 tablespoon kosher salt (Diamond Crystal or about half as much Morton)

Get your oven to 400°F.

Poke a few holes in the skins of the sweet potatoes, put on a baking sheet, and bake until they're nice and soft all the way through, about 1 hour.

Meanwhile, peel, core, and cut the apples into ½-inch pieces. In a medium pan over medium heat, cook the apples with 2 tablespoons of the butter until they turn golden brown and lose their crunch, about 20 minutes. Move the mixture to your food processor; add the cinnamon, allspice, and cloves; and set aside.

When the sweet potatoes are done, combine the heavy cream, remaining 7 tablespoons butter, maple syrup, and salt in the medium pan over medium heat and warm, stirring occasionally, until the butter melts. Add the mixture to the food processor on top of the apples and buzz it all on high speed until smooth, about 1 minute.

With a spoon, scoop the hot sweet potato flesh into the food processor; discard the skins. Buzz, stirring and scraping occasionally, until smooth. Taste and add more salt, if you want. Serve in something pretty.

This will also keep in your fridge for 5 days or so.

USED TO CALL IT STUFFING, NOW I CALL IT DRESSING

I remember the first time that I hosted my family for Thanksgiving. I was a young cook with big ideas about what made food cool. I cooked for hours, churning out butternut squash gratin, churched-up collards, and stuffing made with kohlrabi brunoise, duxelles of mushrooms, and dried sour cherries. You can really follow my evolution as a cook by looking at the stuffing from those first five Thanksgivings. I started at showy and ended at Stove Top—but you know, the good homemade Stove Top.

Now I go somewhere in the middle and make this stuffing (or dressing, since I live in Louisiana), and I will keep making it forever. There are big flavors from a few key ingredients—winter herbs, meat from chicken wings, and juicy porky nugs of Jimmy Dean. It has all the pleasures of my fancy attempts but none of the pomp. It's my second favorite dish on the table every November, and that's only because my mom's burnt tomatoes (see page 165) will forever reign supreme. My hope is that sharing this recipe helps break whatever national puritanical fever has convinced us that stuffing should be made only once a year.

SERVES 8 TO 10

6 to 8 hot dog buns, cut into ½-inch cubes (8 cups)

1¾ pounds (about 6) whole chicken wings

2 teaspoons kosher salt (Diamond Crystal or about half as much Morton)

1 pound loose breakfast sausage (like Jimmy Dean)

4 tablespoons unsalted butter

1 yellow onion, cut into small dice

4 celery stalks, cut into small dice

5 garlic cloves, minced

1 cup buttermilk

2 tablespoons finely chopped rosemary

2 tablespoons finely chopped sage

2 tablespoons chopped thyme

Heaping 1 tablespoon granulated chicken bouillon (preferably Totole brand, see page 110; optional but optimal)

2 teaspoons freshly ground black pepper

½ teaspoon cayenne pepper

2 eggs

Get your oven to 250°F.

Bake the bun cubes on a baking sheet until they're dry and brittle all the way through, 30 minutes (depending on the brand and freshness of the buns). Take them out and set them aside.

Turn your oven temp to 425°F.

Season the chicken wings with 1 teaspoon of the salt, put them in a 9 by 13-inch casserole dish along with 2 cups water, and bake, uncovered, until they bust a little at the seams and the parts of the wings that aren't submerged turn light cardboard brown, 70 to 80 minutes.

Take the casserole dish out of the oven but leave the oven on. Tip the liquid into a measuring cup. You want at least ½ cup, so top it off with water if need be. Let the wings hang out until they're cool enough to handle, then pick the meat off the bones into little bits and put them in the mixing bowl. Eat the skin as you go because it's delicious but won't be an awesome texture in the stuffing.

While the wings cook, brown the sausage in a medium skillet over medium-high heat, stirring and breaking it up into little pieces, until it's cooked through, about 5 minutes. Scoop the sausage into the mixing bowl, leaving any fat behind. Lower the heat to medium; add the butter, onion, celery, and garlic; and cook, stirring, until the onion is translucent and the celery has just a bit of crunch left, 10 minutes or so. Scrape it all into the mixing bowl.

Go ahead and add the remaining 1 teaspoon salt, the buttermilk, rosemary, sage, thyme, chicken bouillon, black pepper, cayenne, and eggs to the bowl. Mix it all together, then add the bun cubes and mix until they're all wet.

Butter that casserole dish, add the stuffing mix in an even layer, and cover tightly with foil. Bake at 425°F for 40 minutes on the center rack, then remove the foil and keep baking until the top gets nice and brown and the center is hot and steamy, 10 to 15 minutes more.

Serve the stuffing, but call it dressing.

SCOTTY'S GOOD-WITH-EVERYTHING COLLARD GREENS

These days, Scotty Yelity makes the best pot of collard greens at Turkey and the Wolf. He stews them for a good long while with butter, garlic, and vinegar until they're real soft. We use them for The Collard Melt (page 106) at Turkey and the Wolf and pile them on top of grits (see page 18) at Molly's Rise and Shine. And even though we love ham and bacon, we don't use any here—they just don't need any.

Collards cooked this way were a mini milestone in my career, the first thing I riffed on as a young cook at Coquette that earned me a "fuck yeah" from my boss—and a bit of kitchen autonomy that let me pursue creations of my own.

Of course, my collards were never exactly mine. They were adapted from whoever taught the person who taught the person who first showed me. And it's important to sit with the fact that I wouldn't be cooking or eating collard greens if not for the legacy of enslaved Africans. Jessica B. Harris's *High on the Hog: A Culinary Journey from Africa to America* is a great place to read more on this.

**SERVES 4 TO 6
(MAKES ABOUT 6 CUPS)**

4 bunches collard greens (about 10 ounces each)

6 tablespoons unsalted butter

6 to 8 garlic cloves, finely chopped

5 tablespoons white sugar

⅓ cup red wine vinegar, or more if you like

⅓ cup unseasoned rice vinegar

⅓ cup Louisiana-style hot sauce

1 tablespoon plus 2 teaspoons Zatarain's Creole Seasoning, or more if you like

1 tablespoon gochugaru (Korean chile flakes) or other red chile flakes

2 teaspoons granulated chicken bouillon (preferably Totole brand, see page 110; optional but optimal)

2 teaspoons kosher salt (Diamond Crystal or about half as much Morton), or more if you like

Tear the leaves from the stems of the collards, discarding the stems, and chop into 1- to 2-inch pieces. You'll have about 10 cups, packed. Set them aside for a sec.

Melt the butter in a large, heavy pot over medium heat. Add the garlic and cook, stirring, until fragrant but not browned, about 1 minute. Add the sugar, red wine and rice vinegars, hot sauce, Creole seasoning, chile flakes, chicken bouillon, and salt along with 8 cups water. Turn the heat to high to bring the mixture to a simmer and cook for a minute or two, so the flavors meld and develop.

In a few batches, add the collard greens, stirring and letting them wilt a bit before adding the next batch. When you've added all the collards, crank up the heat to bring it all to a simmer, then adjust the heat to maintain a low simmer. Cook until they're nice and soft (you might even say a bit mushy) and, just as important, the liquid has reduced to a rich, heavenly broth (this is pot likker, if you didn't already know) that's an inch or so deep, about 2½ hours. Season with more salt, Creole seasoning, and red wine vinegar until you're happy, then simmer for another couple of minutes.

Serve hot or let the collards cool in the pot likker, transfer to an airtight container, and keep in the fridge for up to 1 week.

THERE SHOULD PROBABLY BE A SALAD (CAESAR)

Hell no, I'm not going to write a book of my favorite recipes and not put a Caesar salad in there. It's my go-to for the compulsory bit of greenery on the loaded holiday table. And while I typically love messing up the classics, this Caesar is pretty straightforward, especially compared to the other salads on my ranch. The lettuce is romaine. The dressing is a flavor bomb of lemon and anchovy, garlic and Parm, and jarred mayo. And I go huge on the croutons made from hot dog buns, because that's what Liz does and she's in charge of baking, even when that means re-baking grocery store buns.

To make the dressing: Buzz the anchovies, garlic, oil, mustard, Worcestershire sauce, pepper, salt, the finely grated zest of 1 lemon, and the juice of 1½ lemons in a blender on high speed until smooth-ish, about 30 seconds. Pour it into a medium mixing bowl, add the mayo and Parm, and mix real well. Taste and add more lemon juice until you're happy.

The dressing makes about 1½ cups and keeps in the fridge for a couple of weeks.

To make the croutons: Get your oven to 300°F.

Toss the bun cubes with the oil in a medium mixing bowl to get them all evenly coated. Add the garlic powder, salt, and pepper and toss again.

Spread the cubes evenly on a baking pan and bake them, rotating the pan once halfway through, until they're Winnie-the-Pooh brown and crunchy to the core, 30 to 40 minutes.

To assemble the salad: Put the romaine in a big honking bowl with 1 cup of the dressing (or more—I like it overdressed) and the juice of the lemon. Use your hands to toss well so the lettuce is nicely coated, then add most of the cheese and the croutons and toss again. Add the rest of the cheese, and go to crank town with a pepper grinder, if you want. Serve with the onion slices, if desired, and those anchovies laying on top, or for dangling over friends' heads and then slowly lowering into their mouths like I imagine ancient Roman nobility ate grapes.

SERVES 6 TO 8

Dressing

8 to 10 oil-packed anchovy fillets, drained

3 medium garlic cloves

3 tablespoons extra-virgin olive oil

1 tablespoon Dijon mustard

1 teaspoon Worcestershire sauce

1 teaspoon freshly ground black pepper

½ teaspoon kosher salt (Diamond Crystal or about half as much Morton)

2 juicy lemons

1 cup mayo (Duke's or bust)

3 ounces real Parm, finely grated (1 cup)

Croutons

8 hot dog buns, cut into 1-inch cubes

⅓ cup extra-virgin olive oil

1½ tablespoons garlic powder

1 teaspoon kosher salt (Diamond Crystal or about half as much Morton)

1 teaspoon freshly ground black pepper

Salad

4 hearts of romaine, trimmed and torn into 2-inch pieces

1 juicy lemon

3 ounces real Parm, finely grated (1 cup)

Coarsely ground black pepper

1 cup thinly sliced red onion (optional)

More of those nice anchovies (optional)

THE MAMA TRIED BURGER

A few times a year, we host a dog and burger pop-up called Mama Tried, named for the Merle Haggard song (Nate's favorite) and the Grateful Dead's cover (mine). Either way, we both thought it would make a great name for a restaurant.

This is how we do the burgers, and a few little details make them awesome. First is straight Lawry's, no salt or pepper. Second, we use two thin patties, which mean double cheese and more surface area for that Lawry's. Third, we cook those patties in a pan, not on a grill, so they bathe in their juices, rather than losing them to the fire. And last, those juices get mopped up with a potato bun from Martin's, the best in the world. I also really like that the patties don't have much of a crust so that the crunch and texture come from the classic burger toppings.

Set a medium cast-iron skillet over high heat until it's pretty hot. While the skillet's heating up, put a beef ball between two pieces of parchment or wax paper and evenly flatten it to make a 6-inch patty. Repeat with the other ball on separate parchment paper.

Add about ½ teaspoon of the butter to the pan and swirl it around. Lower the heat to medium, then add one of the patties and season the up-side liberally with Lawry's (a generous ¼ teaspoon per patty).

Cook until the first side gets a little brown (you're not looking for a crust here), 30 to 45 seconds. Flip the patty, add a cheese slice, and cook until the cheese starts to melt, about 45 seconds more.

Move the patty to a plate and use a roll half to wipe up the buttery drippings, leaving it for a few seconds, so it gets a little toasty. Cook the other patty the same way (the butter, the Lawry's, the slice of cheese), but this time, stack the patty on the other patty. Use the other roll half to sop up the drippings and let it get toasty, too.

Now you can go wild, but here's how I make each one: Swipe some mayo (couple of teaspoons or so) on one half of the roll and some ketchup on the other half. Add the patty stack to the bottom, then top with the lettuce, tomato, some onion, pickle chips, and the roll top. Eat.

MAKES 1 AWESOME DOUBLE CHEESEBURGER

5 ounces ground beef, divided into two 2-inch balls

1 teaspoon unsalted butter

Generous ½ teaspoon Lawry's Seasoned Salt

2 slices American cheese

1 Martin's potato sandwich roll

Mayo (Duke's or bust) for swiping

Ketchup (there is only Heinz) for swiping

2 bun-size pieces iceberg lettuce

2 thin tomato slices

Some thinly sliced white or yellow onion

4 or so drained dill pickle chips

DAN STEIN AS A HOT DOG

Dan Stein is my friend, mentor, and spiritual advisor. He's kind, strong, and devastatingly handsome. He officiated my wedding. He inspired The Collard Melt (page 106). When I told him I was opening a sandwich shop just down the street from his sandwich shop, Stein's Deli, he didn't slash my tires—he bought me a deli slicer. Here, I present Dan—who's a little salty, a little spicy, a little meaty, and spends a lot of time around rye bread—as an anthropomorphized hot dog.

MAKES 4

4 hot dogs (I love Hebrew National all-beef), or Corned Dog Upgrade (page 188)

1½ cups drained sauerkraut

1 white onion, cut into thin half-moons

1 teaspoon kosher salt (Diamond Crystal or about half as much Morton)

4 tablespoons unsalted butter, room-temp so it's mayo-soft

2 ounces sliced Swiss cheese

4 slices soft rye bread (preferably marble or seeded)

¼ cup Spicy Russian Dressing (page 225)

Ketchup (there is only Heinz) for serving

Heaping ¼ cup chopped hot pickled cherry peppers

Cook the dogs however you like to cook your dogs (microwave, grill, skillet) or do what we do at Turkey and the Wolf (see Corned Dog Upgrade, page 188). Keep them warm.

Combine the sauerkraut, onion, salt, and 1 tablespoon of the butter in a medium nonstick pan or well-seasoned cast-iron skillet and put it over medium heat. Cook, stirring with a wooden spoon, occasionally at first and more frequently near the end, until the kraut and onion turn golden brown, about 5 minutes. Add the cheese and let it melt, about 1 minute. Turn off the heat and stir well. Cover to keep warm.

Get a well-seasoned cast-iron skillet or griddle good and hot over medium heat. Swipe the remaining 3 tablespoons butter generously on the rye slices. Working in batches, if necessary, toast the bread in the skillet until it's golden brown but still soft enough to fold like a bootleg bun, 30 seconds or so. Move the bread to plates or a platter.

Spoon a nice long stripe of the Russian dressing along the center of each slice of rye and squeeze on a thin stripe of ketchup right next to it. Top with the hot dogs, the cheesy sauerkraut, and the pickled peppers. Eat it like a hot dog.

CORNED DOG UPGRADE

POWER-UP

Not to be confused with Via's corn dogs (see page 191), this method gives your wieners an awesome Reuben-esque quality.

(see page 191)

MAKES 4

Combine 8 cups water and the salt, peppercorns, coriander seeds, allspice berries, and cloves in a medium pot and get it to a boil. Let it cool fully, pour it into a container, and add the hot dogs. Refrigerate overnight or up to 2 days.

When you're ready to eat the dogs, dump it all into a pot, bring it to a simmer, and turn off the heat. Serve as desired.

1 tablespoon kosher salt (Diamond Crystal or about half as much Morton)

1 tablespoon black peppercorns

1 tablespoon coriander seeds

1 tablespoon allspice berries

1 tablespoon whole cloves

4 hot dogs (I love Hebrew National all-beef)

THE OFFICIAL HOT DOG OF THE WORCESTER HOT DOG SAFARI

The city of Worcester, Massachusetts, has an annual wiener expedition called the Hot Dog Safari. I know this because of my pal Bob, Turkey and the Wolf cook and Worcester native, is one of the hosts along with the true Safari luminary, Tom Mahoney, a.k.a. Hot Dog Tom. Google it. It's a super-cool event, and the money they make from selling the handsome merch gets donated to the local food bank. Since Bob and his friends helped create the Safari, they got to bestow the title of its official dog. And it went to this number, born from a camping trip where the person responsible for condiment procurement fucked up and only brought peanut butter. It acquired a ketchup upgrade later on, when me, Bob, and the fam were working the menu for a Mama Tried pop-up and we had a eureka moment when someone busted out the Heinz. Not everyone can get down to this boogie, but I sure do.

Cook the dogs hot by any means necessary—in a microwave, steamer, or oven, or on a radiator—though they're extra good charred on a hot grill.

Stick them in some toasty buns and spoon on about 1 tablespoon peanut butter and squirt on about half that amount of ketchup per dog. Taste the magic.

DAN
STEIN

VIA'S CORN DOGS WITH HER MOM'S MUSTARD

My former roommate and dear friend Via Fortier is a real Renaissance woman, always on the grind. Her side hustles include selling taxidermy and vintage Saints gear, as well as serving as Turkey and the Wolf's online merch lady. She also helped run a boar sausage company, was a dog-treat chef, and launched a great burger joint, where she created a corn dog that will live on in my heart forever (and lives on here in this recipe). You won't find a better one at the county fair or Mardi Gras (at least not without help from mood enhancers). The best way to eat it is with her mom Tay's extraordinarily dank mustard.

MAKES 6

Vegetable oil for deep-frying (about 2 quarts)

6 regular hot dogs

2 cups all-purpose flour

1 cup fine yellow cornmeal

¼ cup white sugar

1½ teaspoons baking powder

1 teaspoon baking soda

1 teaspoon kosher salt (Diamond Crystal or about half as much Morton)

1¼ cups well-shaken buttermilk

1 egg, lightly beaten

Tay's Mustard (page 217) or your favorite sweet-hot mustard for serving

Get your oven to 250°F and line a baking sheet with a wire rack or paper towels. Put about 2 inches of oil in a heavy pot or Dutch oven and set it over medium-high heat until it registers 350°F on a deep-fry or candy thermometer.

While the oil is heating up, slide a long wooden skewer into each dog, stopping before the point pokes through the dog. Dump 1 cup of the flour onto a large plate, then roll the hot dogs around to coat them in the flour, shaking off any excess.

In a medium mixing bowl, combine the cornmeal, sugar, baking powder, baking soda, salt, and remaining 1 cup flour, stir well, then add the buttermilk and egg and whisk until smooth. Pour it into a tall glass for easy battering.

When the oil reaches 350°F, dip one dog into the batter to evenly coat it, giving the skewer a quarter twirl as you lift it out, so any excess batter drips off.

Holding it by the skewer as close to parallel to the oil as you can without maiming yourself, dip the dog in the oil and keep it there for 10 seconds, then carefully drop it into the oil. Repeat—batter, dip, and drop—for two or three more dogs, depending on the size of your pot. You don't want to overcrowd and you want a little space between each one.

Fry the first batch, flipping them over halfway through (about 5 minutes) if they don't flip themselves over and adjusting the heat to maintain the oil temperature, until the crust has a nice grocery-bag brown color and a cake tester or paring knife inserted into the batter (but not the dog) comes out clean and warm to the touch, 8 to 10 minutes. Move them to the baking sheet, pop in the oven to keep them warm, and fry the rest in batches, adding them to the baking sheet as they're done. Serve with sweet-hot mustard.

NOT YO MAMA'S PEANUT BUTTER-BACON BURGER

On those occasions when the classic cocktail of hallucinogens and bourbon had me adventuring downriver and toward the bright lights and stiff, sugary daiquiris of the French Quarter, I always ended up in the sweet embrace of Yo Mama's. It's closed now, but this busy, dingy bar and grill sold a peanut butter–and–bacon burger that I'd get every damn time. It sounds like a gimmick, but in fact, it's scientifically proven that joining savory beef fat, salty cured pork, and creamy peanut butter makes everything feel right. Fuck a Tempur-Pedic—if you want comfort, make this burger.

MAKES 1 AWESOME BURGER

5 ounces ground beef, divided into two 2-inch balls

1 teaspoon unsalted butter

Generous ½ teaspoon Lawry's Seasoned Salt

1 Martin's potato sandwich roll

2 bun-size pieces iceberg lettuce

Some thinly sliced red onion

Creamy peanut butter for serving

2 strips bacon, cooked however you like your bacon

Ketchup (there is only Heinz) for swiping

Set a medium cast-iron skillet over high heat until it's pretty hot. While the skillet's heating up, put a beef ball between two pieces of parchment or wax paper and evenly flatten it to make a 6-inch patty. Repeat with the other ball on separate parchment paper.

Add about ½ teaspoon of the butter to the pan and swirl it around. Lower the heat to medium, then add one of the patties and season the up-side liberally with Lawry's (a generous ¼ teaspoon per patty).

Cook until the first side gets a little brown (you're not looking for a crust here), 30 to 45 seconds. Flip the patty and cook about 45 seconds more.

Move the patty to a plate and use a roll half to wipe up the buttery drippings, leaving it for a few seconds, so it gets a little toasty. Cook the other patty the same way (the butter, the Lawry's), but this time, stack the patty on the other patty. Use the other roll half to sop up the drippings and let it get toasty, too.

Here's how I build it, but no rules apply, as long as you get all the stuff between the buns: On the bun bottom, add the lettuce leaf and some onion. Add the patty stack, then some peanut butter (I go large and use 3 tablespoons, but 2 tablespoons is probably more reasonable) and the bacon (break 'em up to fit on the burger). Swipe some ketchup on the top bun, cap the burger, and eat.

SPICY CHICKEN THIGH ROASTER SANDWICH

This guy and the one on page 197 are essentially the same but hit different. They both get brined and dosed with spicy spices, but somehow rubbing the mix on before roasting and sprinkling it on after frying produces two distinct dimensions of poultry-on-a-squishy-bun goodness. It's proof that science is real. The toppings are pretty much same-same—mayo and pickles, iceberg, and an indispensable squeeze of lemon—except for the French's Crispy Fried Onions that give this roasted one some crunch.

Chicken

¼ cup kosher salt (Diamond Crystal or about half as much Morton)

2 tablespoons white sugar

4 boneless skinless chicken thighs (about 1½ pounds total)

¼ cup Nate's Spicy Chicken Spices (page 230)

½ juicy lemon

Sandwiches

4 teaspoons unsalted butter, room-temp so it's mayo-soft

4 Martin's potato sandwich rolls

Mayo (Duke's or bust) for swiping

8 bun-size pieces iceberg lettuce

12 to 16 drained dill pickle chips

1 cup French's Crispy Fried Onions

To brine and roast that chicken:
Up to 12 hours or as little as 2 hours ahead, brine the chicken. Combine 4 cups water with the salt and sugar in a medium pot and set it over medium heat. Stir occasionally, just until the sugar and salt dissolve, then let it cool completely. If you've got the space in your fridge, stick the chicken thighs in the pot so they're submerged in the brine and put it in the fridge. Otherwise, put the thighs and brine in a resealable bag and seal it.

Get your oven to 400°F.

Drain the chicken, pat it dry, and season all over with the chicken spices. Roast on a baking sheet until the center is cooked through (just cut into it and peek inside), about 15 minutes. Immediately squeeze on the lemon juice and let the chicken hang out while you toast your rolls.

To assemble those sandwiches:
Get a well-seasoned cast-iron skillet or griddle good and hot over medium heat.

Swipe ½ teaspoon butter onto the cut side of each roll half, then cook the cut sides in batches until they're dark golden brown. It goes quick, like 30 seconds to 1 minute. When they're done, move them to the counter to build your sandwich.

If the chicken thighs are big, cut them to fit on the rolls. Evenly swipe about 1 teaspoon mayo on each roll half. On each roll bottom, pile 2 lettuce leaves, 3 or 4 pickle chips, the chicken, and then ¼ cup of the fried onions. Top with the other half of the roll and go at it. Simple but awesome.

NATE'S SPICY FRIED CHICKEN SANDWICH

It's important to note that the sophisticated crunch and crackle of this sandwich—an upgrade of the one of page 194—is essentially the result of Michael Solomonov letting me use the cornstarch batter recipe he uses for the fried chicken at his restaurant Federal Donuts.

To brine that chicken: Heat 4 cups water with the salt and sugar in a medium pot, stirring occasionally, just until they dissolve, then let cool completely. Add the chicken so it's submerged (or put the chicken and brine in a big resealable bag) and put it in the fridge for at least 2 hours or up to 12 hours.

To fry that chicken: An hour or so before you're ready to fry, drain the chicken, pat it dry, and let it come to room temp. Then get 2 inches of oil to 350°F in a medium heavy pot.

While your oil heats up, whisk together the cornstarch, flour, black pepper, salt, cayenne, garlic powder, and 1 cup water in a medium bowl.

When the oil's hot, one by one, dunk each thigh in the batter, so it's fully coated, then carefully add to the oil. To keep them from sticking to the pot or one another, I add two thighs to the oil, wait 2 or 3 minutes, then add the other two. Fry them, adjusting the heat to maintain 325-ish°F, until the crust is super-crackly and light brown and the center is cooked through (just cut into it and peek inside), about 15 minutes.

When the thighs are done, pull them from the oil with tongs, shaking off any excess oil, and move them to a mixing bowl. Immediately and evenly sprinkle with the chicken spices, tossing to get as much of it to stick as possible. Let them hang out in the bowl.

To assemble those sandwiches: Get a well-seasoned cast-iron skillet or griddle good and hot over medium heat.

Swipe ½ teaspoon butter onto the cut side of each roll half, then cook the cut sides in batches until they're dark golden brown. It goes quick, like 30 seconds to 1 minute. When they're done, move them to the counter to build your sandwich.

Evenly swipe about 1 teaspoon mayo on each roll half. On each roll bottom, pile on 2 lettuce leaves, 3 or 4 pickle chips, and the chicken. Squeeze a generous spritz of lemon juice onto the chicken on each sandwich and top with the other half of the roll. Eat. I love this sandwich.

MAKES 4

For Brining the Chicken

¼ cup kosher salt (Diamond Crystal or about half as much Morton)

2 tablespoons white sugar

4 boneless skinless chicken thighs (about 1½ pounds total)

For Frying the Chicken

Vegetable oil for deep-frying (about 2 quarts)

1 cup cornstarch

½ cup all-purpose flour

2 teaspoons freshly ground black pepper

1 teaspoon kosher salt (Diamond Crystal or about half as much Morton)

¼ teaspoon cayenne pepper

½ teaspoon garlic powder

Heaping ¼ cup Nate's Spicy Chicken Spices (page 230)

Sandwiches

4 teaspoons unsalted butter, room-temp so it's mayo-soft

4 Martin's potato sandwich rolls

Mayo (Duke's or bust) for swiping

8 bun-size pieces iceberg lettuce

12 to 16 drained dill pickle chips

½ juicy lemon

HOW TO MAKE A FRENCH-FRY
*OR ANYTHING ELSE FRIED
SANDWICH

This one's not exactly a recipe, since homemade fries are for the birds and the rest is as much guidance as it is instruction. Plus, if you have our herb mayo and Via's mom's mustard hanging around in your fridge, you're prepared to turn practically anything fried into a really good sandwich.

Sweet-hot mustard and herb mayo are always at Turkey and the Wolf, so we've used these condiments to make sandwiches with fried chicken skins (see page 139) as a special. But since the team likes to eat it but doesn't necessarily want to prep more skins, we tried it with french fries and it was so good I put it in this cookbook. Buy them on your way home and warm them in the oven or buy them frozen and follow the package instructions. Or have it your way: Stuff these with Popeyes leftovers, fish sticks, crispy pig ears (see page 45), or just a handful of potato chips.

Get a heavy skillet hot over medium heat, swipe real-soft butter onto the cut sides of some Martin's potato sandwich rolls, and cook them in batches until they're golden brown. Swipe a heaping teaspoon of sweet-hot mustard (like Tay's, see page 217) on one side of each roll and a heaping teaspoon of Bellair-Style Herb Mayo (page 218) or plain Duke's mayo on the other. Put on some shrettuce (see page 229), sliced red onions, little tender dill sprigs, pickle chips, and then a giant handful of fries. Shake on some Louisiana-style hot sauce. Throw the other half of the roll on top, and you're in business.

Desserts

"LOOKS LIKE IT'S JUST LIQUOR AND DESSERT FROM HERE ON OUT." THAT'S SOMETHING MY DAD, THE LATE ROBERT HEREFORD, USED TO SAY TO DISMISS THE FEAR AND LOATHING OF HARD NEWS FROM THE DOCTOR, AND TO REMIND US THAT WE BEST BE PARTYING; SEEING AS OUR TIME HERE IS LIMITED. HE MANAGED TO KEEP THE PARTY GOING AT A PRETTY FULL TILT UNTIL THE END. HIS COOLNESS CONTINUES TO BE AN INSPIRATION.

I TRY TO KEEP SOME OF THAT SPIRIT ALIVE HERE. SO HAVE FUN AND CRUSH SOME SWEET AFTER-DINNER TREATS EVEN IF YOU, LIKE ME, KNOW NOTHING ABOUT DESSERT COOKERY.

NO-CHURN ICE CREAM SUNDAE

There are few greater bodega-purchased pleasures than the Snickers ice cream bar. It has been crushing its handheld rivals from the year of its blessed birth back in '96. Since then, the only thing separating this titan of frozen treats from the leagues of the fine-dining pastry course is plateware. If you have fancy dishes, now is the time.

I suggest you enjoy this with an extremely stiff bourbon and Coke. Drop a handful of salty peanuts in your cocktail and for a moment, everything seems like it's going to be OK.

MAKES 1 PERFECT DESSERT

3 grocery store–size or 2 gas station–size Snickers ice cream bars

Whipped cream for garnish (optional but optimal)

1 maraschino cherry

In a cereal bowl or whatever bowl you want, mash up the Snickers bars according to your heart's desire. If you have a ripping-cold freezer, you might need to leave them out for a few minutes until they're mashable.

Garnish with whipped cream and the maraschino cherry. Eat with a spoon.

BEET BUTTER AND TAHINI ON ICE CREAM

This one is all Liz Hollinger, the sous chef and pastry whiz at Molly's. She put beet butter on vanilla ice cream and our jaws dropped. A generous drizzle of tahini completes this fun, mega-earthy dessert that tastes more sophisticated than most of our sweets. It's good on scoops of all sorts, but cookies and cream is the move here.

SERVES 1 TO 4

Beet Butter

1 pound trimmed beets

3 tablespoons white sugar

3 tablespoons unsalted butter, softened

½ teaspoon kosher salt (Diamond Crystal or about half as much Morton)

½ teaspoon vanilla extract

For Serving

1 pint cookies 'n cream ice cream

½ cup well-stirred tahini

Flaky sea salt

To make the beet butter: Get your oven to 350°F.

Wrap the beets individually in foil if they're big boys, or wrap a few together if they're small or medium. Roast them on a baking sheet until you can easily pierce the center with a fork, 1½ to 2 hours. Carefully unwrap and let them hang out until they're cool enough to handle.

One by one, hold the beets in a paper towel and rub off and ditch the peels. Combine the beets, sugar, butter, kosher salt, and vanilla in a blender and buzz on high speed until completely smooth, about 1 minute. If you need to, add a splash of water to help it blend.

Pour the contents of the blender into a medium skillet, bring it to a steamy burble over medium heat, and cook, stirring pretty much constantly, for 10 minutes. It'll thicken up a bit. Let it cool and it's ready to use. It keeps in the fridge for up to 10 days.

To serve: Scoop the ice cream into bowls (or just leave in the carton), drizzle on the tahini, spoon a couple of tablespoons of beet butter onto each bowl, and add a pinch of flaky salt. Eat.

MAGIC SHELL AND POTATO STIX ON ICE CREAM

This is for everyone who's ever dipped fries in a milkshake. Homemade (and microwaveable!) magic shell adds class on top of class.

To make the magic shell: Combine the chocolate chips and coconut oil in a double boiler (small pot, inch of simmering water, heat-proof bowl perched on top) and let melt, stirring until smooth. Or nuke them in microwave-safe bowl on high in 30-second intervals, stirring between each go. Give it one more good stir and let it cool to room temp.

It keeps in an airtight container at room temperature for approximately one decade. The surface might look a little dusty, which is normal. Briefly microwave if it solidifies between uses.

To serve: Scoop the ice cream into bowls (or just leave in the carton), spoon on the magic shell however you want, and garnish with a handful of potato sticks and a pinch of salt. Eat.

SERVES 1 TO 4

Magic Shell

1 cup semisweet chocolate chips

3 tablespoons coconut oil

For Serving

1 pint vanilla or chocolate ice cream

4 handfuls of potato sticks (like the Utz brand)

Kosher salt

CRUNK CHUNKS ON ICE CREAM

I think Crunk Chunks were Colleen's idea. Maybe Nate's. Basically, they're key lime pie but with opposite proportions of salty graham cracker crust and tangy lime custard. Regardless, we put them on soft serve when we opened Turkey and the Wolf and they're awesome.

SERVES 2 TO 8

To make the crunk chunks: Get your oven to 350°F.

In a medium mixing bowl, combine the graham cracker crumbs, butter, sugar, and kosher salt and mix it with your hands until it's all like wet sand.

Line a loaf pan with parchment paper so the paper hangs over the sides by an inch or two. Put the graham sand in there and give it a firm press onto the bottom so you have an even packed layer that's a smidge more than an inch. Bake, rotating the pan once, until the edges start to darken a shade but the center isn't quite done, 12 to 15 minutes.

While you're waiting, whisk together the condensed milk, key lime juice, and egg yolks so they're well mixed. When the crust is done, pour on the lime mixture, give the pan a couple of taps on the counter so the lime stuff settles evenly, then bake again until the lime mixture is just barely set in the center, 10 to 12 minutes.

Let this bad boy come to room temperature, then pop it in the fridge until it's cold and it's good to go. It keeps, covered, in the fridge for a week or the freezer for two.

To serve: Run a knife along the edges of the crunk daddy to loosen him from the pan, then use the parchment paper to lift out and cut him into roughly 1-inch crunk chunk babies. Scoop the ice cream into bowls (or just leave in the carton), top with the crunk chunks, and garnish with a pinch of flaky salt. Eat.

Crunk Chunks

One 14.4-ounce box graham crackers (ground to fine bread crumb size)

2 sticks (16 tablespoons) plus 3 tablespoons unsalted butter, melted

½ cup white sugar

1 tablespoon kosher salt (Diamond Crystal or about half as much Morton), or more if you like

¾ cup plus 2 tablespoons sweetened condensed milk

¼ cup bottled key lime juice (like Nellie and Joe's)

2 egg yolks

For Serving

2 pints vanilla, coconut, or Creole cream cheese (a Louisiana thing) ice cream

Flaky sea salt

CANDIED PEANUTS, NUTTER BUTTERS, AND TOASTED COCONUT ON ICE CREAM

Since my dessert cookery skills are nonexistent, I asked my friend Nini Nguyen (of the granola on page 22) to help me with some cool ice-cream toppings, because she is one of those people who's good at making savory stuff, making sweet stuff, and making everyone around her feel special. We decided to include this one to celebrate the recently shuttered Uncle Boon's, where she took me for my first time. We had an unforgettable meal that ended with their toasted coconut sundae with candied peanuts, and for a moment life was perfect. Here's our homage to that dessert and the greatest restaurant there ever was.

SERVES 1 TO 4

Candied Peanuts

1 cup white sugar

2 cups unsalted roasted peanuts

Flaky sea salt

For Serving

½ cup sweetened coconut flakes

1 pint vanilla, coconut, or Jeni's Salted Peanut Butter ice cream

4 Nutter Butters, whacked into pieces

Flaky sea salt

To candy the peanuts: Line a baking sheet with parchment paper. Combine the sugar and ¼ cup water in a medium skillet, give it a stir, and get it bubbling over medium-high heat. Cook, without stirring, until it turns golden brown in some spots, 4 to 5 minutes. Now start paying extra-close attention and keep cooking, swirling the pan frequently but still not stirring, until it turns an even bourbon color, about 1 minute more.

Immediately turn off the heat, add the peanuts and a generous sprinkle of salt, and stir to coat well. Dump it all out onto the baking sheet in a single-ish layer to cool, breaking up any group hugs of polyamorous candied nuts. They'll keep at room temp in an airtight container for up to 1 week.

To serve: Get your oven to 325°F.

Spread the coconut flakes in an even layer on a small baking sheet and toast in the oven, stirring every 2 minutes or so, until they turn Winnie-the-Pooh brown, 6 to 8 minutes. Keep an eye out because they go from zero to brown real quick. Dump them in a bowl to cool.

Scoop the ice cream in bowls (or just leave in the carton). Add the coconut flakes, Nutter Butters, and 1 cup of the peanuts, then finish with a sprinkle of salt. Eat.

CHEEZ-ITS AND PEANUTS ON ICE CREAM

Whenever I pull a tub of ice cream from the freezer, the first thing I do is throw away the lid. Second thing I do is make this. It started with one of my mom's many fine snacking moves, an arsenal that includes sandwiching potato chips around pickle slices, eating Ritz crackers with butter and jelly, and, best of all, putting salty peanuts on ice cream. My contribution is the Cheez-Its addition. I'd say I get down with this dish more often than any other in this book.

Scoop the ice cream into bowls (or just leave in the container). Grab a handful of Cheez-Its and sprinkle them on top, giving it all a scrunch so some get crushed and some stay whole. Add the peanuts and get to it.

SERVES 1 TO 10

1 pint to 1½ gallons ice cream (vanilla, cookies 'n cream, anything really)

Cheez-Its for sprinkling

Salted roasted peanuts for sprinkling

WHEN I DIP, YOU DIP, WE DIP, S

I'VE BEEN A DIP GUY EVER
SINCE I WATCHED MY OLD
MAN DUNK THE LAST BITE
FROM OUR CHILI'S APPETIZER
SAMPLER IN EVERY LAST
SAUCE ON THE TABLE. AND
THERE WERE SIX OF THEM.

VERDANT BLENDER SAUCE

I only hope that you enjoy this half as much as I do the chimichurri at La Boca, my favorite steakhouse in New Orleans. Try it with skirt steak, sweetbreads, or anything, really, from the grill.

MAKES ABOUT 1 CUP

Use a Microplane to zest the lemons into your blender, halve the lemons, and squeeze in about ¼ cup worth of juice. Add the oil, then add the cilantro, parsley, garlic, and salt. Blend on high speed until pretty smooth, about 30 seconds. Season with more salt and lemon juice until you're happy.

This can be made up to half a day ahead of time (keep it in the fridge if you're storing it for more than 2 hours). The next day, it's not as good.

2 juicy lemons, for zesting and juicing

½ cup extra-virgin olive oil

1 bunch cilantro, bottoms trimmed (about 1¾ cups tightly packed)

1 bunch parsley, bottoms trimmed (about 1¾ cups tightly packed)

2 garlic cloves, peeled

1 teaspoon kosher salt (Diamond Crystal or about half as much Morton), or more if you like

TAY'S MUSTARD

A few years back, I was deep into recipe testing for the not-quite-open-yet Turkey and the Wolf when my bud Via came through big time. She sent me a recipe for sweet-hot mustard from her mom, Tay, a caterer by trade and consummate host by temperament. I tried it, I loved it, and our bologna sandwich (see page 126) wouldn't hit without it.

(see page 126)

MAKES ABOUT 1½ CUPS

1 cup distilled
white vinegar

1 cup white sugar

One 4-ounce tin Colman's
mustard powder

1 tablespoon kosher salt
(Diamond Crystal or about
half as much Morton)

3 eggs

Combine the vinegar, sugar, mustard powder, salt, and eggs in a medium heatproof bowl and whisk until smooth.

Pour an inch or so of water into a small saucepan, bring it to a boil over medium-high heat, then lower the heat to medium-low. Set the bowl in the saucepan (without touching the water). Start stirring right away and keep at it, using a rubber spatula to frequently stir and scrape the sides so the eggs don't have the chance to scramble, until the mixture thickens to a consistency that's a bit looser than your average Dijon mustard, about 15 minutes. Give it a good whisk to get rid of any clumps.

Take the bowl off the pan, let the mustard cool, then cover and refrigerate until it's fully chilled, 1 hour or so. It'll thicken a bit more.

Use it now or keep it in an airtight container in the fridge for up to 3 weeks.

BELLAIR-STYLE HERB MAYO

This is essential for The Bellair (page 104), but my wife refers to it as the cure-all for any basic-bitch sandwiches.

MAKES ABOUT 2 CUPS

Mix all the ingredients together in a bowl. Taste and add more salt until you're happy.

It keeps in an airtight container in the fridge for up to 10 days.

2 cups mayo
(Duke's or bust)

¼ cup roughly
chopped dill

2 tablespoons finely
chopped thyme leaves

1½ tablespoons
celery seeds

1 tablespoon Creole
mustard (like Zatarain's)
or whole-grain mustard

1½ teaspoons kosher salt
(Diamond Crystal or about
half as much Morton),
or more if you like

PEANUT BUTTER SALSA MACHA

Daniela Soto-Innes, the former chef at Atla and Cosme in New York, makes my favorite salsa in the world. I love it and I'm grateful she shared it with me (because we make it at the restaurants and put it on everything). Now you can make it, too—if you buy her cookbook *Tu Casa Mi Casa*, which she wrote with Enrique Olvera.

This one can't touch her original, but with her permission, I'm sharing a dilettante's version, a peanut butter interpretation of her rich, nutty, complex, slightly spicy super-condiment that keeps some of the awesomeness intact.

MAKES ABOUT 2½ CUPS

1 cup grapeseed oil or vegetable oil

5 garlic cloves, peeled

8 dried pasilla chiles, stemmed, slit open, and seeded

12 dried arbol chiles, stemmed, slit open, and seeded

1 cup chunky peanut butter (the natural stuff!)

2 teaspoons kosher salt (Diamond Crystal or about half as much Morton)

Combine the oil and garlic in a small, heavy pot (narrow enough so the oil submerges the garlic). Turn the heat to medium-high and cook until the garlic is golden brown, 5 to 7 minutes. Use a slotted spoon to move the garlic to a bowl. Leave the oil in the pot and keep the heat on.

Add the pasilla chiles, two or three at a time (they cook really quick, so be ready) to the hot oil and fry, holding them under with a strainer and using the strainer to pull them out as soon as they blister, 5 to 10 seconds. As they're done, move them to the bowl with the garlic. Fry the arbol chiles in the same way until they darken slightly, 5 to 10 seconds, then move them to the bowl.

Let the oil cool to warm, pour it into a food processor, and add the garlic and chiles. Buzz for about 20 seconds, then add the peanut butter and salt and buzz until pretty smooth, another 15 to 30 seconds. Now it's done.

It keeps in the fridge for up to 2 weeks.

**VERDANT
BLENDER SAUCE**
(PAGE 216)

**SPICY
RUSSIAN DRESSING**
(PAGE 225)

BELLAIR-STYLE HERB MAYO
(PAGE 218)

NINI'S GRANOLA
(PAGE 22)

**ANCHOVY
CRÈME FRAÎCHE**
(PAGE 224)

**HALFWAY-HOMEMADE
HOT SAUCE**
(PAGE 222)

PEANUT BUTTER SALSA MACHA
(PAGE 219)

TAY'S MUSTARD
(PAGE 217)

**NATE'S SPICY
CHICKEN SPICES**
(PAGE 230)

**BIG ZESTY
BUTTERMILK DRESSING**
(PAGE 226)

PEA MAKEOVER
(SEE PAGE 73)

CHICKEN SALT
(PAGE 231)

**GAS-STATION
BEAN DIP**
(PAGE 227)

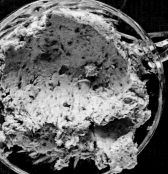

**PIZZA
CREAM
CHEESE**
(PAGE 223)

HALFWAY-HOMEMADE HOT SAUCE

I considered not even telling y'all how we make Turkey and the Wolf's hot sauce. I've worked in kitchens where I'd be laughed at for it. But I see a sort of glory in the half-assedness of it all. Because if something tastes awesome and you had fun, well then congratulations. So here it is.

Combine the vinegar, sugar, salt, garlic, jalapeño, carrot, onion, and 2 cups water in a medium pot over medium-high heat and bring it to a boil. Lower the heat and let simmer, stirring once or twice, until the onion is translucent, the carrot is soft, and the jalapeño has faded like your go-to jeans, 25 minutes or so.

Move everything to your blender (liquid and all), add all the hot sauces, and blend until smooth.

It'll keep the fridge for a month or two.

MAKES ABOUT 2 CUPS

½ cup distilled white vinegar

2½ tablespoons white sugar

1½ teaspoons kosher salt (Diamond Crystal or about half as much Morton)

2 garlic cloves, peeled

1 jalapeño, stemmed and roughly chopped

½ carrot, peeled and roughly chopped

¼ yellow or white onion, roughly chopped

¼ cup Crystal hot sauce

¼ cup Huy Fong Foods Sriracha

2 tablespoons Valentina hot sauce

PIZZA CREAM CHEESE

Colleen's intention in making this was evoking Bagel Bites. She succeeded, though she also created an umami-ass spread with all sorts of applications, from cheesy meatloaf bagels (see page 32) to giving garlic bread some French bread pizza pizzazz. Her original uses sliced tomatoes dried overnight in a low oven, but we reworked it with sun-dried tomatoes so y'all can make it in a jiffy.

MAKES ABOUT 1½ CUPS

Combine the sun-dried tomatoes and oil, garlic, oregano, chicken bouillon, salt, pepper, and 2 tablespoons water in your blender and blend on high speed to make a chunky paste, about 1 minute.

Move the mixture to a food processor or a mixing bowl and add the cream cheese. Pulse or stir until smooth-ish and well mixed.

It keeps in the fridge for up to 2 weeks or until the expiration date on the cream cheese.

¾ cup drained oil-packed sun-dried tomatoes, plus 1 tablespoon of the oil

1 tablespoon dried minced garlic

1½ teaspoons dried oregano

1½ teaspoons granulated chicken bouillon (preferably Totole brand, see page 110; optional but optimal)

1¼ teaspoons kosher salt (Diamond Crystal or about half as much Morton)

1 teaspoon freshly ground black pepper

8 ounces (1 cup) Philadelphia cream cheese, room-temp so it's nice and soft

ANCHOVY CRÈME FRAÎCHE

Just like the word "buttermilk" in a title makes something sound delicious, crème fraîche makes everything sound fancy—even when it's not. This rich, tangy dollop for hash browns (see page 94), spoonbread (see page 85), and potato chips contains zero French-style cultured cream. But it turns out the combination of sour cream, cream cheese, and lemon tastes pretty crème fraîche–y. Anchovies give it a magical savoriness, and here, high-quality anchovy brands, like Ortiz, Angostino Recca, and Agromar, keep things in balance.

Combine the sour cream, lemon juice, salt, and anchovies (including their oil) in a blender and blend until smooth. Add the cream cheese in several blobs (it's easier on your blender that way) and pulse just until it's all smooth (blend too much and it'll be too loose, but still good). If you want, add more salt and lemon juice.

It keeps in the fridge for up to 1 week or until the expiration date on the sour cream or cream cheese.

MAKES ABOUT 1 CUP

½ cup sour cream

¼ cup fresh lemon juice (from about 2 lemons), or more if you like

¼ teaspoon kosher salt (Diamond Crystal or about half as much Morton), or more if you like

One 2-ounce can oil-packed anchovy fillets

4 ounces (½ cup) Philadelphia cream cheese, room-temp so it's nice and soft

SPICY RUSSIAN DRESSING

We swap in hot cherry peppers for the typical pickles in Russian dressing and add just a whisper of ketchup along with hot sauce and chile flakes. Few sandwiches on Earth can resist its charms, but it's designed for The Collard Melt (page 106) and moonlights on the Dan Stein dog (see page 186).

Combine all the ingredients, stir, then season with more salt until you're happy.

It keeps in the fridge for up to 2 weeks.

MAKES A HEAPING 1 CUP

1 cup mayo (Duke's or bust)

½ cup roughly chopped drained hot pickled cherry peppers (from a jar)

2 teaspoons ketchup (there is only Heinz)

1 teaspoon gochugaru (Korean chile flakes) or other red chile flakes

½ teaspoon Louisiana-style hot sauce

¼ teaspoon kosher salt (Diamond Crystal or about half as much Morton), or more if you like

¼ teaspoon freshly ground black pepper

¼ teaspoon smoked paprika

BIG ZESTY BUTTERMILK DRESSING

Named for my great buddy Richard Horner, who is also big and zesty, this sauce and Richard are otherwise unaffiliated. The dressing has only a trivial affiliation with buttermilk, as you can see, but people eat with their ears as well as their eyes, and you can't tell me that hearing "buttermilk" doesn't evoke wonderful things, like steamy biscuits and ranch from the lushest and most hidden of valleys. Plus, if we called it "big zesty mayo," it could technically refer to half the shit we make.

MAKES ABOUT 1 CUP

½ cup mayo
(Duke's or bust)

½ cup sour cream

2 tablespoons buttermilk

1 tablespoon plus
1 teaspoon fresh lemon
juice, or more if you like

2 teaspoons gochugaru
(Korean chile flakes) or
other red chile flakes

2 teaspoons Zatarain's
Creole Seasoning

½ teaspoon kosher salt
(Diamond Crystal or about
half as much Morton),
or more if you like

½ teaspoon freshly ground
black pepper

Mix all the ingredients together well. If you want, add more salt and lemon.

It keeps in the fridge for up to 10 days.

GAS-STATION BEAN DIP

One of my moves as a kid looking for good snacks on the fly was hitting the chip aisle for that yellow-and-blue can of Fritos bean dip. This recipe scratches the same itch with very little work, plus you can say, Hey, that was delicious, it probably wasn't as bad for me, and I made it myself.

MAKES ABOUT 2 CUPS

One 16-ounce can refried beans

1 tablespoon Tabasco Chipotle Pepper Sauce

2 teaspoons Tabasco Green Pepper Sauce

1 teaspoon chili powder

Juice of ½ lime, or more if you like

Kosher salt

Mix all the ingredients together in a bowl and add salt and more lime juice until you're happy.

It keeps in the fridge for up to 10 days.

MY BEST TRY AT COLLEEN'S ONION DIP

The chef de cuisine at Molly's, opening chef de cuisine of Turkey and the Wolf, and proud new owner of a sour-cream gun, Colleen Quarls is a dip whisperer. Her onion dip is rich and dynamic and nuanced and also slightly above my skill level. So I present you with one that follows her cues while cutting a few corners. It tastes great on tostadas (see page 67) and equally nice on Ritz or Club Crackers.

(see page 67)

MAKES ABOUT 2½ CUPS

1 tablespoon
unsalted butter

1 tablespoon vegetable oil

2 medium yellow onions,
thinly sliced

1½ teaspoons
Worcestershire sauce

1 cup (8 ounces)
Philadelphia cream
cheese, room-temp
so it's nice and soft

1 cup sour cream

1 tablespoon dried
minced garlic

2 teaspoons onion powder

1½ teaspoons kosher salt
(Diamond Crystal or about
half as much Morton)

½ teaspoon freshly ground
black pepper

1 teaspoon granulated
chicken bouillon
(preferably Totole brand,
see page 110; optional
but optimal)

1½ tablespoons Louisiana-
style hot sauce

1 tablespoon fresh lemon
juice, or more if you like

First, combine the butter and oil in a large heavy skillet and set it over medium heat. When the butter melts and sizzles, add the onions, stir, and lower the heat to medium-low. Cook, stirring once in a while at the beginning but more frequently as the onions take on color so they cook evenly and don't stick to the skillet, until they turn a rich dark brown, 1 to 1½ hours. Stir in the Worcestershire sauce and scrape up any brown bits. Let it cool.

Scrape the contents of the skillet into your food processor, add the rest of the ingredients, and buzz until pretty smooth, 30 seconds to 1 minute. In the off chance your food processor struggles in the beginning, pulse the mixture a few times, then continue.

It keeps in the fridge for up to 1 week.

SHRETTUCE

In the years leading up to opening Turkey and the Wolf, I took a ton of notes in my phone, half-formed ideas for when it came time to open the restaurant. They ranged from "Don't forget how smoked potatoes taste with black garlic re: Bar Tartine" to "eBay sells vintage salt and pepper shakers by the lot." But perhaps the one that has served us the best just read "SHRETTUCE!"

So, yeah, I wrote a recipe for how to shred lettuce. It's important. Shrettuce reminds me of the sandwiches I had growing up. It's real crunchy but, almost as important, its flavor doesn't distract from the main event.

MAKES 4 TO 6 CUPS

1 head (¾ to 1 pound) iceberg lettuce

Remove the iceberg head's hearty stem by whacking that sucker stem-side down on the counter. Or just cut the stem off. That's fine, too, but not as much fun. Either way, definitely remove the outermost leaves, which are usually kinda busted.

Using your favorite knife, a tool that's close to your heart for an ingredient that's close to mine, cut the head of lettuce in half through the part where the stem was, then slice each half into thin shreds. Now you have shrettuce.

It keeps in the fridge for a day or two.

NATE'S SPICY CHICKEN SPICES

This is chef de cuisine Nate's gift to chicken lovers, reimagined for easy home use. It's great sprinkled on before roasting (see page 194), after frying (see page 197), and also whenever (see page 143).

MAKES ABOUT 1 CUP

You want the chicken bouillon to be the texture of sand, so grind it up however you like (spice grinder, mortar and pestle, put it in a sealed bag and whack it) and sprinkle it into a bowl. Add the other stuff and mix well, breaking up any clumps.

How long do spices last? That's how long this lasts.

1 tablespoon granulated chicken bouillon (preferably Totole brand, see page 110; optional but optimal)

¼ cup Lawry's Seasoned Salt

¼ cup packed dark brown sugar (or light if that's what you've got)

3 tablespoons cayenne pepper

3 tablespoons smoked Spanish paprika

2 tablespoons kosher salt (Diamond Crystal or about half as much Morton)

1 tablespoon freshly ground black pepper

CHICKEN SALT

Thanks to my bud Nini, everything in my life can taste a little more like chicken, which is probably my favorite flavor. Years ago, she was kind enough to take me shopping at Hong Kong Food Market on the West Bank. When we walked past a row of yellow-and-green canisters emblazoned with a self-possessed chicken in an apron, she basically insisted I put one in my cart. It was Totole brand granulated chicken flavor soup base mix, her favorite brand and now mine, too. Mixed with salt, it bolsters the natural poultry power of pocket pies (see page 133) and conjures wondrous illusions for chicken-fried steak (see page 109) straight from the fryer.

MAKES ABOUT ¾ CUP

½ cup granulated chicken bouillon (preferably Totole brand, see page 110; optional but optimal)

¼ cup kosher salt (Diamond Crystal or about half as much Morton)

You want the chicken bouillon to be the texture of sand, so grind it up however you like (spice grinder, mortar and pestle, put it in a sealed bag and whack it). No biggie if it's a little too coarse or too fine. Stir it together with the salt.

This stuff will last longer than your pantry.

VIA
FORTIER

ADOLFO GARCIA

SCOTTY
YELITY

ACKNOWLEDGMENTS

Thanks, Mom! You got four kids that are now adults and actually friends with each other, an amazing feat that I attribute fully to your superpowers. None of this shit would be happening without your support and the support of Will, Molly, and Saint. Thanks for thrifting all the tables, chairs, and cups we needed to get the restaurant open, and driving with them in a two-story pile on the back of your semi-broken-down pickup truck for fifteen hours in the rain to get them to New Orleans. And thanks for all the other stuff, too.

There are only two things that money can't buy and that's true love and homegrown tomatoes; and if I had to choose, fuck tomatoes. There ain't nothing in this world without my wife, Lauren Agudo. Thank you for sharing your time with me in this lifetime. Plus, thanks for all the stuff you do to make sure the restaurants keep rolling down the track. I'll tell ya the rest in person. And thanks to our dog, Darla. Darla is just so great.

Thank you to my brothers and sister. Will, making a book with you as the photographer is a dream come true. Thank you for absolutely killing it, and for letting me use your K2 Fatty roller-blades occasionally when I still had TRS Lightnings, which is a pretty good metaphor for all you've given to me. Saint, I know your waist is slender, your fingers, they are small, but it would not make you tremble to see ten thousand fall in Super Street Fighter II on Sega Genesis. Thank you for putting a strong wit out into the ether for me to strive to emulate. Molly, you're the best Hereford. Thanks for inspiring an entire restaurant and helping me with everything I've ever written, including papers in college when you were in tenth grade. And thanks for the free therapy.

The most massive thank you to Liz Hollinger, Phil Cenac, Kate Mirante, Nate Barfield, Will Mondros, Scotty Yelity, Bob O'Donnell, Migdalia Pabon, Leticia Alarado, Michael "Swade" Swadener, Sarah Roberts, Mac Folger, Chris Lorio, Colleen Quarls, Daniel Bourgeois, Jess Stokes, Ian Willson, Andrew Dupuis, Nadia, Brett, Gail, Caroline, Savannah, Amber, Josh, Mikey, Kevin, Miriam, Christin, Bronwen, Thelma, Wayne, and everyone else that has ever shared their world with Turkey and the Wolf and Molly's Rise and Shine. It ain't me. You guys are it.

To Lauren Holton, Turkey and the Wolf would never have taken off without you. Your cocktails were effortlessly cool and so are you, and I know people didn't show up those first few months to see me, so I owe ya one.

To Via Fortier, the host of the party. I'm not sure there are enough pages to list your contributions to the restaurants and to my memory bank of good times. Let's go out to dinner tomorrow. And thank your mom for me, for creating you and for all the recipes. They're pure gold.

To Kim Witherspoon and the team at Inkwell for believing that I could write a cookbook and then making sure some publishers did, too.

To the team at Ten Speed Press, especially Kelly Snowden, Emma Rudolph, and Betsy Stromberg, for buying that cookbook and patiently and thoughtfully helping me create something that I'm really fucking proud of.

To JJ Goode for telling me I should write a cookbook and then actually writing the cookbook, even though you don't understand how to properly use the word "y'all" in a sentence. Seriously though, I wouldn't have gotten down this road without you.

To Shavon for delivering smiles and bread and lighting up the room when you walk in and always wearing our merch.

To Leighann and Dan for making the bologna before you had a place to make it and then continuing to make it after you opened a busy-ass butcher shop that didn't need to be making it, and for being our pals.

To Toure Folkes for your friendship and for helping us grow.

To Dan Stein for being my light.

To Nini Nguyen for being such a good friend, for sharing recipes and pastry knowledge, for charting our path through Hong Kong Food Market, and for showing me my favorite parts of NYC.

To Ashtin Berry for your friendship, advice, leadership, lessons, shopping suggestions, and conversations over too many drinks.

To Remy Robert for expertly testing the recipes and providing much needed input.

BLAZE WILLIAMS

PRINCE LOBO

To Matty Matheson for doing the all-caps things on Instagram, which I copied and probably helped me get a book deal.

To Joe Trippi and Zane Gould for teaching me to cook the first stuff I ever cooked. To Chris Shortall and Mike Stoltzfus for teaching me the second stuff I ever cooked. And to everyone at Coquette.

To Ashlee Arceneaux Jones for the lettering in this book, the eye for design, the "order here" sign at Turkey and the Wolf, the undertaking that was the sign at Molly's, and, most important, being my bud. I can't imagine how this book would look without you. You're amazing.

To David Weiss for manufacturing the shit out of our white bread for us, for putting up with wild bread orders, and always having a backup ready to go.

To Michael Solomonov for letting me copy off his hummus and chicken homework.

To Ann Redding and Matt Danzer of Uncle Boon's for providing endless inspiration to this fanboy.

To Leo Gonzales for the illustrations in this book and so many more. You crush so hard every time. To Kenny Cox for the murals at both restaurants, merch, designs, and half my tattoos, including the one that led to an FDA investigation of whether we were running a tattoo shop out of the restaurant. To Stewart Freeman for being the first ever Turkey and the Wolf illustrator and for that time you shaved your head like Friar Tuck and I laughed myself into astral projection. To Seth Fountain, Paul Portis, and Meep for amazing design work.

To Danny and Bonnie's Seafood for having the best cracklin, to Rahman Mogilles and the McHardy's team for having the best fried chicken, to Adolfo Garcia and La Boca for having the best steak, to Quoc Trieu and the Tan Dinh team for having the best fish-sauce wings and short ribs, to Tiffany Higgins for having the best crabmeat, to Nina Compton for having the best game nights (and food), to Prince Lobo and Addis NOLA for having the best beef tibs. And once more to everyone in this paragraph for being a supportive friend.

To the late Julia Reed for showing us what cool looks like and always being there for us.

To Ryan Pfeiffer, Elaine Marisol, and the Big Kids Staff.

To Tom Bielskas, our most reliable customer. To Brian Gibbs for being our most generous customer. To JJ Redick for being the regular customer that's best at basketball.

To Jennifer Coolidge for being so cool and so generous and so supportive.

To Kemper, Delia, and Mike Maupin for creating and running my childhood home base.

To Southern Solidarity for being there for our unhoused New Orleans neighbors.

To Michael Jordan, Steve Irwin, and Beyoncé.

And finally to Robert Hereford, my old man. Thank you. You're the reason I have a mustache. You're the reason I always have Guy Clark and the Grateful Dead stuck in my head. You're why I like drinking beer out of a small glass. My memories of you are a fucking blessing.

COLLEEN QUARLS

NINA COMPTON

ABOUT THE AUTHORS

MASON HEREFORD is the owner (and depending on who you ask, sorta the chef) of Turkey and the Wolf in New Orleans, a counter-service sandwich joint that *Food & Wine* and *GQ* magazines, both called one of the most important restaurants of the decade. He also owns Molly's Rise and Shine, a breakfast spot nearby that *Food & Wine* listed as a Best New Restaurant in America. He credits any success to his colleagues who constantly inject their character into the restaurant. Mason was born and raised on rollerblades in rural Virginia; he now lives in New Orleans and will never leave.

JJ GOODE helps people write books, and mostly cookbooks, which are the best books. He has coauthored several *New York Times* bestsellers and has been nominated for several James Beard Awards. He writes essays and articles sometimes, too. The editors of *The Norton Reader* selected his *Gourmet* magazine essay on cooking with one arm for their anthology of nonfiction, which includes writing from Nora Ephron, Barack Obama, and Jesus.

INDEX

A

American cheese, 32
anchovies
    Anchovy Crème Fraîche, 224
    There Should Probably Be a
        Salad (Caesar), 181
apples
    Buffalo Waldorf Salad, 39
    Mason's Danksgiving Day
        Puree, 172
    My Best Attempt at Anne
        Hereford's Apple Fritters, 171

B

bacon
    Not Yo Mama's Peanut Butter–
        Bacon Burger, 192
    The Wedge, 53
beans
    Double-Decker Boomtown
        Upgrade, 68
    Gas-Station Bean Dip, 227
    White Bean Hummus with
        Chile-Crunch Peas, 65
beef
    The 86'd Chicken-Fried Steak,
        109–10
    how to steak, 158
    The Mama Tried Burger, 184
    Meatloaf: The Bagel, Not the
        Musician, 32–33
    Meatloaf: The Meatloaf, Not the
        Musician, 33
    Meatloaf: The Sandwich, Not
        the Musician, 129
    Not Yo Mama's Peanut Butter–
        Bacon Burger, 192
    slicing steak, 109
beets
    Beet Butter and Tahini on Ice
        Cream, 205
Bellair-Style Herb Mayo, 218
The Bellair (The Reason We Make
    Sandwiches), 104–05

Big Zesty Buttermilk Dressing, 226
Bird Sauce, 112
Biscuits, Molly's, 25–26
Blue Cheese Dressing, Chunky, 54
The Bologna, 126
bread
    about, 102–03
    There Should Probably Be a
        Salad (Caesar), 181
    Used to Call It Stuffing, Now
        I Call It Dressing, 176–77
breakfast
    Collards and Grits with Salsa
        Macha, 18
    Colleen's Bagel Bites, 17
    Country Gravy Upgrade, 28
    Deviled-Egg Tostadas, 14
    Don't Sleep on the Carrot
        Yogurt, 21
    Grand Slam McMuffin, 30–31
    Liz's Carrot Marmalade, 23
    Meatloaf: The Bagel, Not the
        Musician, 32–33
    Molly's Biscuits, 25–26
    Nini's Granola, 22
Buffalo Waldorf Salad, 39
burgers
    The Mama Tried Burger, 184
    Not Yo Mama's Peanut Butter–
        Bacon Burger, 192
Burnt Tomatoes, Mom's Famous,
    165–66
Burrito, Sweet Potato, 61
butter, soft-ass, 125
buttermilk
Buttermilk Dressing, Big Zesty, 226
Buttermilk Mashed Potatoes, 167

C

cabbage
    The Cabbage Patch, 42
    The Collard Melt, 106
Caesar salad
    There Should Probably Be a
        Salad (Caesar), 181

Candied Peanuts, Nutter Butters,
    and Toasted Coconut on
    Ice Cream, 210
Candied Walnuts, 40
carrot juice
    Liz's Carrot Marmalade, 23
carrots
    Chicken Potpies That Fit in
        Your Pocket, 133–34
    Don't Sleep on the Carrot
        Yogurt, 21
Catfish Blues, 79
celery
    Buffalo Waldorf Salad, 39
    Chicken Potpies That Fit in Your
        Pocket, 133–34
    Used to Call It Stuffing, Now
        I Call It Dressing, 176–77
cheese
    American cheese, 32
    The Bellair (The Reason We
        Make Sandwiches), 104–05
    Chunky Blue Cheese
        Dressing, 54
    The Collard Melt, 106
    Feta Cream Cheese, 72
    Grand Slam McMuffin, 30–31
    Hog's Head Cheese Tacos, 154
    The Mama Tried Burger, 184
    Meatloaf: The Bagel, Not the
        Musician, 32–33
crackers
    Cheez-Its and Peanuts on Ice
        Cream, 213
chicken
    Chicken Potpies That Fit in Your
        Pocket, 133–34
    Chicken Salt, 231
    chicken skins, 140
    Fried Chicken Skins and
        Deviled Eggs, 139–40
    Leftover Fried Chicken Salad, 47
    Nate's Spicy Chicken
        Spices, 230

chicken, continued
  Nate's Spicy Fried Chicken
    Sandwich, 197
  Spicy Chicken Thigh Roaster
    Sandwich, 194
  Spicy Fried Chicken Salad on
    Roti Paratha, 143
  Used to Call It Stuffing, Now
    I Call It Dressing, 176–77
chicken bouillon, granulated
  about, 110
  Chicken Salt, 231
Chicken-Fried Steak, The 86'd,
  109–10
chiles
  Chipotle Romesco, 88
  Coconut-Chile Dressing, 44
  Green Taco Sauce, 138
  Hot Tuna, 91
  Peanut Butter Salsa Macha, 219
  Shrimp with Grapes and
    Nuts, 97
  Spiced Chile Paste, 146
Chimichurri Cream Cheese, 93
Chipotle Romesco, 88
chocolate
  Magic Shell, 206
cilantro
  Corner-Store Pork Rind
    Tacos, 137
coconut flakes
  Candied Peanuts, Nutter
    Butters, and Toasted
    Coconut on Ice Cream, 210
coconut milk
  Coconut-Chile Dressing, 44
collard greens
  The Collard Melt, 106
  Collards and Grits with Salsa
    Macha, 18
  Hog's Head Cheese
    Collards, 157
  Scotty's Good-With-Everything
    Collard Greens, 178
Colleen's Bagel Bites, 17
Colleen's Onion Dip, My Best
  Try at, 228
corn
  Roe a la Jiffy, 85
Corn Dogs, Via's, with Her Mom's
  Mustard, 191
Corned Dog Upgrade, 188
Corner-Store Pork Rind
  Tacos, 137

corn tortillas
  Corner-Store Pork Rind
    Tacos, 137
  Hog's Head Cheese Tacos, 154
  Strippies, 155
Country Gravy Upgrade, 28
crab
  buying and cleaning
    softies, 124
  Crab Cake Muffs, 82
  The Softshell Crab, 123
  Sunday Morning Coming-Down
    Potato Salad, 50
Cracklins Upgrade, Pig Ear, 45
cream cheese
  Anchovy Crème Fraîche, 224
  Chimichurri Cream Cheese, 93
  Colleen's Bagel Bites, 17
  Feta Cream Cheese, 72
  Gas-Station Tostadas, 67
  Italian-Sandwich Cream
    Cheese, 120
  My Best Try at Colleen's Onion
    Dip, 228
  Pizza Cream Cheese, 223
  Roasted Sunchoke and White
    Truffle Dunkaroos, 62
  Sweet Potato Burrito, 61
  Visualize Whirled Peas on
    Toast, 71
Crunk Chunks on Ice Cream, 209
cucumbers
  Shrimp with Grapes and
    Nuts, 97
cutting board salad, 115

D

Dan Stein as a Hot Dog, 186
deep-frying, 41
deli meat
  The Bellair (The Reason We
    Make Sandwiches), 104–05
  The Bologna, 126
  The Italian-American, 119
dessert
  Beet Butter and Tahini on
    Ice Cream, 205
  Candied Peanuts, Nutter
    Butters, and Toasted
    Coconut on Ice Cream, 210
  Cheez-Its and Peanuts on
    Ice Cream, 213
  Crunk Chunks on Ice
    Cream, 209

Magic Shell and Potato Stix on
  Ice Cream, 206
No-Churn Ice Cream
  Sundae, 202
deviled eggs
  Deviled-Egg Tostadas, 14
  Fried Chicken Skins and
    Deviled Eggs, 139–40
dips and spreads. See also sauces
  Anchovy Crème Fraîche, 224
  Bellair-Style Herb Mayo, 218
  Bird Sauce, 112
  Chimichurri Cream Cheese, 93
  Chipotle Romesco, 88
  Feta Cream Cheese, 72
  Gas-Station Bean Dip, 227
  Green Taco Sauce, 138
  Grocery-Store Tonnato
    Sauce, 161
  Italian-Sandwich Cream
    Cheese, 120
  Malt Vinegar Tartar Sauce, 124
  My Best Try at Colleen's Onion
    Dip, 228
  Peanut Butter Salsa Macha, 219
  Pizza Cream Cheese, 223
  Spiced Chile Paste, 146
  Spicy Russian Dressing, 225
  Tastes-Like-There's-Gravy-In-It-
    Mayo, 129
  Tay's Mustard, 217
  White Bean Hummus with
    Chile-Crunch Peas, 65
  White Truffle Dunkaroos,
    Roasted Sunchokes and, 62
Don't Sleep on the Carrot
  Yogurt, 21
Dorito Dust, 68
Double-Decker Boomtown
  Upgrade, 68
dressing
  Used to Call It Stuffing, Now I
    Call It Dressing, 176–77
dressing, salad
  Big Zesty Buttermilk
    Dressing, 226
  Chunky Blue Cheese
    Dressing, 54
  Coconut-Chile Dressing, 44
  Italian-Sandwich
    Vinaigrette, 120
  Spicy Russian Dressing, 225
Duke's mayonnaise, 112

E

The 86'd Chicken-Fried Steak, 109–10
eggs
    Deviled-Egg Tostadas, 14
    Fried Chicken Skins and
        Deviled Eggs, 139–40

F

Feta Cream Cheese, 72
fish and seafood
    Catfish Blues, 79
    Crab Cake Muffs, 82
    Grocery-Store Tonnato
        Sauce, 161
    Hot Tuna, 91
    How We Eat Sardines, 93
    Lobster Tostadas, 86
    McCaviar, 94
    Roe a la Jiffy, 85
    Shrimp with Grapes and
        Nuts, 97
    The Softshell Crab, 123
fish eggs
    McCaviar, 94
    Roe a la Jiffy, 85
french-fry sandwiches, 199
fried chicken
    Fried Chicken Skins and
        Deviled Eggs, 139–40
    Leftover Fried Chicken Salad, 47
    Spicy Fried Chicken Salad on
        Roti Paratha, 143
Fritters, My Best Attempt at Anne
    Hereford's Apple, 171
fruit
    Don't Sleep on the Carrot
        Yogurt, 21
    Mason's Danksgiving Day
        Puree, 172
    My Best Attempt at Anne
        Hereford's Apple Fritters, 171

G

Gas-Station Bean Dip, 227
Gas-Station Tostadas, 67
gochugaru, 44
graham crackers
    Crunk Chunks on Ice
        Cream, 209
Grand Slam McMuffin, 30–31
Granola, Nini's, 22
grapes
    Shrimp with Grapes and
        Nuts, 97

Gravy Upgrade, Country, 28
Green Taco Sauce, 138
grits
    Collards and Grits with Salsa
        Macha, 18
Grocery-Store Tonnato Sauce, 161

H

Halfway-Homemade Hot
    Sauce, 222
ham
    The Bellair (The Reason We
        Make Sandwiches), 104–05
hash brown patties
    Grand Slam McMuffin, 30–31
    McCaviar, 94
head cheese
    hog head's cheese itinerary,
        150–51
    Hog's Head Cheese, 147–48
    Hog's Head Cheese
        Collards, 157
    Hog's Head Cheese Rice, 153
    Hog's Head Cheese Tacos, 154
hog head's cheese
    hog head's cheese itinerary,
        150–51
    Hog's Head Cheese, 147–48
    Hog's Head Cheese Collards, 157
    Hog's Head Cheese Rice, 153
    Hog's Head Cheese Tacos, 154
hot dogs
    Corned Dog Upgrade, 188
    Dan Stein as a Hot Dog, 186
    Via's Corn Dogs with Her Mom's
        Mustard, 191
    Worcester Hot Dog Safari, 188
Hot Sauce, Halfway-
    Homemade, 222
Hot Tuna, 91
How We Eat Sardines, 83
Hummus with Chile-Crunch Peas,
    White Bean, 65

I

ice cream
    Beet Butter and Tahini on Ice
        Cream, 205
    Candied Peanuts, Nutter
        Butters, and Toasted
        Coconut on Ice Cream, 210
    Cheez-Its and Peanuts on
        Ice Cream, 213
    Crunk Chunks on Ice
        Cream, 209

Magic Shell and Potato Stix on
    Ice Cream, 206
    No-Churn Ice Cream
        Sundae, 202
The Italian-American, 119
Italian-Sandwich Cream
    Cheese, 120
Italian-Sandwich Vinaigrette, 120

J

Jimmy Dean sausage, 31

K

kale
    Catfish Blues, 79
key lime juice
    Crunk Chunks on Ice
        Cream, 209

L

lamb
    Lamb, Peas, Mint, and Cereal
        Salad, 57
    Slow-Cooked Lamb Necks
        with Fixings on Roti Paratha,
        145–46
Leftover Fried Chicken Salad, 47
lettuce
    Shrettuce, 229
Liz's Carrot Marmalade, 23
Lobster Tostadas, 86

M

Magic Shell and Potato Stix on Ice
    Cream, 206
Malt Vinegar Tartar Sauce, 124
The Mama Tried Burger, 184
Marmalade, Liz's Carrot, 23
Mashed Potatoes, Buttermilk, 167
Mason's Danksgiving Day Puree, 172
mayonnaise
    Bellair-Style Herb Mayo, 218
    Bird Sauce, 112
    Duke's mayonnaise, 112
    Malt Vinegar Tartar Sauce, 124
    Spicy Russian Dressing, 225
    Tastes-Like-There's-Gravy-In-It-
        Mayo, 129
meatloaf
    Meatloaf: The Bagel, Not the
        Musician, 32–33
    Meatloaf: The Meatloaf, Not the
        Musician, 33
    Meatloaf: The Sandwich, Not
        the Musician, 129

mint
   Lamb, Peas, Mint, and Cereal
      Salad, 57
Molly's Biscuits, 25–26
Mom's Famous Burnt Tomatoes,
   165–66
Mustard, Tay's, 217
My Best Attempt at Anne
   Hereford's Apple Fritters, 171
My Best Try at Colleen's Onion
   Dip, 228

N

Nate's Spicy Chicken Spices, 230
Nate's Spicy Fried Chicken
   Sandwich, 197
Nini's Granola, 22
No-Churn Ice Cream Sundae, 202
Not Yo Mama's Peanut Butter–
   Bacon Burger, 192
nuts
   Candied Peanuts, Nutter
      Butters, and Toasted
      Coconut on Ice Cream, 210
   Candied Walnuts, 40
   Cheez-Its and Peanuts on Ice
      Cream, 213
   Chipotle Romesco, 88
   Lamb, Peas, Mint, and Cereal
      Salad, 57
   Nini's Granola, 22
   Shrimp with Grapes and Nuts, 97

O

oats
   Nini's Granola, 22
okra
   Okranomiyaki, 75
Onions
   My Best Try at Colleen's Onion
      Dip, 228

P

peanut butter
   Not Yo Mama's Peanut Butter–
      Bacon Burger, 192
   Peanut Butter Salsa Macha, 219
peanut butter sandwich cookies
   Candied Peanuts, Nutter
      Butters, and Toasted
      Coconut on Ice Cream, 210
peanuts
   Candied Peanuts, Nutter
      Butters, and Toasted
      Coconut on Ice Cream, 210

Cheez-Its and Peanuts on Ice
   Cream, 213
peas
   Lamb, Peas, Mint, and Cereal
      Salad, 57
   making over frozen peas, 73
   Visualize Whirled Peas on
      Toast, 71
   White Bean Hummus with
      Chile-Crunch Peas, 65
Pickled Sweet Peppers, 153
Pig Ear Cracklins Upgrade, 45
Pizza Cream Cheese, 223
pork
   hog head's cheese itinerary,
      150–51
   Hog's Head Cheese, 147–48
   Hog's Head Cheese
      Collards, 157
   Hog's Head Cheese Rice, 153
   Hog's Head Cheese Tacos, 154
   Pig Ear Cracklins Upgrade, 45
pork rinds
   Corner-Store Pork Rind
      Tacos, 137
potatoes
   Buttermilk Mashed
      Potatoes, 167
   Sunday Morning Coming-Down
      Potato Salad, 50
potato sticks
   Magic Shell and Potato Stix on
      Ice Cream, 206
potpies
   Chicken Potpies That Fit in Your
      Pocket, 133–34

R

rice
   Hog's Head Cheese Rice, 153
Rice Krispies
   Lamb, Peas, Mint, and Cereal
      Salad, 57
Roasted Sunchoke and White
   Truffle Dunkaroos, 62
Roe a la Jiffy, 85
Romesco, Chipotle, 88
roti paratha
   about, 135
   Chicken Potpies That Fit in Your
      Pocket, 133–34
   Slow-Cooked Lamb Necks
      with Fixings on Roti Paratha,
      145–46

Spicy Fried Chicken Salad on
   Roti Paratha, 143
Russian Dressing, Spicy, 225

S

salads
   Buffalo Waldorf Salad, 39
   The Cabbage Patch, 42
   cutting board salad, 115
   Lamb, Peas, Mint, and Cereal
      Salad, 57
   Leftover Fried Chicken
      Salad, 47
   Sunday Morning Coming-Down
      Potato Salad, 50
   There Should Probably Be a
      Salad (Caesar), 181
   The Wedge, 53
Salsa Macha, Peanut Butter, 219
Salt, Chicken, 231
sandwiches
   The Bellair (The Reason
      We Make Sandwiches),
      104–05
   The Bologna, 126
   bread, 102–03
   Catfish Blues, 79
   The Collard Melt, 106
   Colleen's Bagel Bites, 17
   Crab Cake Muffs, 82
   The 86'd Chicken-Fried Steak,
      109–10
   french-fry sandwiches, 199
   Grand Slam McMuffin, 30–31
   The Italian-American, 119
   Meatloaf: The Bagel, Not the
      Musician, 32–33
   Meatloaf: The Sandwich, Not
      the Musician, 129
   Nate's Spicy Fried Chicken
      Sandwich, 197
   Slow-Cooked Lamb Necks
      with Fixings on Roti Paratha,
      145–46
   The Softshell Crab, 123
   Spicy Chicken Thigh Roaster
      Sandwich, 194
   Spicy Fried Chicken Salad on
      Roti Paratha, 143
   Sweet Potato Burrito, 61
   The Tomato, 116–17
   Visualize Whirled Peas on
      Toast, 71
Sardines, How We Eat, 93

sauces. *See also* dips and spreads
  Green Taco Sauce, 138
  Grocery-Store Tonnato
    Sauce, 161
  Halfway-Homemade
    Hot Sauce, 222
  Spiced Chile Paste, 146
  Verdant Blender Sauce, 216
sausage
  Country Gravy Upgrade, 28
  Grand Slam McMuffin, 30–31
  Jimmy Dean, 31
  Used to Call It Stuffing, Now I
    Call It Dressing, 176–77
Scotty's Good-With-Everything
  Collard Greens, 178
seafood. *See* fish and seafood
Shrettuce, 229
Shrimp with Grapes and Nuts, 97
side dishes
  Buttermilk Mashed
    Potatoes, 167
  Mason's Danksgiving Day
    Puree, 172
  Mom's Famous Burnt Tomatoes,
    165–66
  My Best Attempt at Anne
    Hereford's Apple Fritters, 171
  Scotty's Good-With-Everything
    Collard Greens, 178
  There Should Probably Be a
    Salad (Caesar), 181
  Used to Call It Stuffing, Now I
    Call It Dressing, 176–77
  Slow-Cooked Lamb Necks with
    Fixings on Roti Paratha,
    145–46
soft-ass butter, 125
The Softshell Crab, 123
sour cream
  Anchovy Crème Fraîche, 224
  My Best Try at Colleen's Onion
    Dip, 228
  Roe a la Jiffy, 85
spice blends
  Chicken Salt, 231
  Nate's Spicy Chicken
    Spices, 230
Spiced Chile Paste, 146
Spicy Chicken Thigh Roaster
  Sandwich, 194
Spicy Fried Chicken Salad on Roti
  Paratha, 143
Spicy Russian Dressing, 225

spoonbread
  Roe a la Jiffy, 85
Steak
  The 86'd Chicken-Fried Steak,
    109–10
  how to steak, 158
  slicing, 109, 158
Strippies, 155
stuffing
  Used to Call It Stuffing, Now I
    Call It Dressing, 176–77
sunchokes
  Roasted Sunchoke and White
    Truffle Dunkaroos, 62
Sunday Morning Coming-Down
  Potato Salad, 50
sun-dried tomatoes
  Pizza Cream Cheese, 223
sweet peppers
  Pickled Sweet Peppers, 153
sweet potatoes
  Leftover Fried Chicken
    Salad, 47
  Mason's Danksgiving Day
    Puree, 172
  Sweet Potato Burrito, 61

T

tacos
  Corner-Store Pork Rind
    Tacos, 137
  Green Taco Sauce, 138
  Hog's Head Cheese Tacos, 154
tahini
  Beet Butter and Tahini on Ice
    Cream, 205
Tartar Sauce, Malt Vinegar, 124
Tastes-Like-There's-Gravy-In-It-
  Mayo, 129
Tay's Mustard, 217
There Should Probably Be a Salad
  (Caesar), 181
tomatillos
  Corner-Store Pork Rind
    Tacos, 137
The Tomato, 116–17
tomatoes
  Mom's Famous Burnt Tomatoes,
    165–66
  The Tomato, 116–17
  The Wedge, 53
tomatoes, sun-dried
  Pizza Cream Cheese, 223
Tonnato Sauce, Grocery-Store, 161

toppings
  Dorito Dust, 68
  Strippies, 155
tostadas
  Deviled-Egg Tostadas, 14
  Double-Decker Boomtown
    Upgrade, 68
  Gas-Station Tostadas, 67
  Lobster Tostadas, 86
tuna
  Grocery-Store Tonnato
    Sauce, 161
  Hot Tuna, 91

U

Upgrade
  Corned Dog, 188
  Country Gravy, 28
  Nate's Spicy Fried Chicken
    Sandwich, 143, 197
  Pig Ear Cracklins, 42, 45
Used to Call It Stuffing, Now I Call
  It Dressing, 176–77

V

Verdant Blender Sauce, 216
Via's Corn Dogs with Her Mom's
  Mustard, 191
Vinaigrette, Italian-Sandwich, 120
Visualize Whirled Peas on Toast, 71

W

Walnuts, Candied, 40
The Wedge, 53
White Bean Hummus with Chile-
  Crunch Peas, 65
White Truffle Dunkaroos, Roasted
  Sunchoke and, 62

Y

yogurt
  Don't Sleep on the Carrot
    Yogurt, 21
  Slow-Cooked Lamb Necks
    with Fixings on Roti Paratha,
    145–46

Ten Speed Press and the Ten Speed Press colophon are registered
trademarks of Penguin Random House LLC.

Library of Congress Cataloging-in-Publication Data
    Names: Hereford, Mason, author. | Goode, JJ, author. | Hereford,
        William, photographer.
    Title: Turkey and the Wolf: flavor tripping in New Orleans / Mason
        Hereford with JJ Goode; photographs by William Hereford.
    Description: First edition. | California: Ten Speed Press, [2022] |
        Includes index.
    Identifiers: LCCN 2021017837 (print) | LCCN 2021017838 (ebook) |
        ISBN 9781984858993 (hardcover) | ISBN 9781984859006 (ebook)
    Subjects: LCSH: Cooking—Louisiana—New Orleans. | Cooking,
        American—Southern style. | Cooking, American—Louisiana style.
        | Turkey and the Wolf (Restaurant)
    Classification: LCC TX715.2.L68 H47 2022 (print) | LCC TX715.2.L68
        (ebook) | DDC 641.59763/35—dc23
    LC record available at https://lccn.loc.gov/2021017837
    LC ebook record available at https://lccn.loc.gov/2021017838

Hardcover ISBN: 978-1-9848-5899-3
eBook ISBN: 978-1-9848-5900-6

Printed in China

Acquiring editor: Kelly Snowden
Production editors: Emma Rudolph, Doug Ogan, and Sohayla Farman
Editorial assistant: Zoey Brandt
Art director and designer: Betsy Stromberg
Production designers: Mari Gill and Faith Hague
Production manager: Dan Myers
Prepress color managers: Nick Patton and Zoe Tokushige
Photo retoucher: Tammy White
Copyeditor: Leda Scheintaub
Proofreader: Mikayla Butchart
Indexer: Amy Hall
Publicist: Kristin Casemore
Marketer: Chloe Aryeh

10 9 8 7 6 5 4 3 2

First Edition

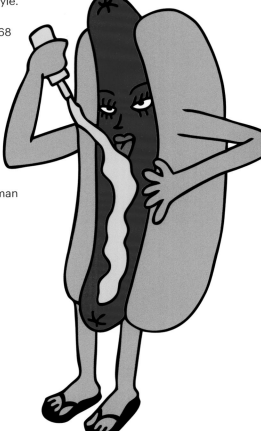